Managing voluntary and non-profit organizations

Strategy and structure

Richard J. Butler

and

David C. Wilson

R

Routledge
London and New York

First published 1990
by Routledge
11 New Fetter Lane, London EC4P 4EE

Simultaneously published in the USA and Canada
by Routledge
a division of Routledge, Chapman and Hall, Inc.
29 West 35th Street, New York, NY 10001

Phototypeset in 10pt Times by
Mews Photosetting, Beckenham, Kent
Printed and bound in Great Britain by
Mackays of Chatham PLC, Chatham, Kent

British Library Cataloguing in Publication Data

Butler, Richard J. *1938–*
    Managing Voluntary and non-profit organizations:
    Strategy and structure
    1. Non-profit making organizations & voluntary
    organizations. Management
    I. Title II. Wilson, David C. *1951–*
    658′.048

Library of Congress Cataloging in Publication Data
also available

ISBN 0-415-02667-9
ISBN 0-415-02668-7 (Pbk)

Contents

Contents

Contents

Figures

Tables

Tables

Preface

This book has a long history and is largely the result of a congruence of research interest in the voluntary sector by the two authors. Richard Butler's interest sprang initially from his work into markets and hierarchies examining the ways in which service provision was allocated throughout the wider economy. David Wilson's perspective came from an interest in alternative organizational structures and the questions of organizational culture and change these debates brought with them. Both authors had previously been engaged in a large-scale study of decision making at the University of Bradford Management Centre, so the seeds for co-authorship were already well embedded.

The project really began as a small part of an ESRC grant which was to examine markets and hierarchies. The voluntary sector was seen as one alternative way of service provision. This project was to employ Susan Saxon-Harrold who began her research work for a Ph.D at the University of Bradford. She was later to become a Research Associate before taking up a post with the Charities Aid Foundation in London. Susan's Ph.D research took her into seventy-five voluntary organizations in Britain and, at the time, represented one of the largest surveys conducted from the perspective of organization theory.

During this time, we were fortunate to be successful in gaining a three-year research grant from the Leverhulme Trust for more detailed study into the strategies and structures of voluntary organizations. This book represents the fruition of these studies.

During the research it soon became apparent that a large-scale survey of the voluntary sector was beyond our scope, such was the variety and number of voluntary organizations. We limited our sample, therefore, to three broad areas of voluntary activity comprising Third World Overseas Aid, Visually Handicapped, and Sea Rescue Services. Following Susan Saxon-Harrold's departure to join the Charities Aid Foundation, we were joined by Jo Dyer as a Research Associate and she became instrumental in much of the detailed empirical work contained in the pages of this book. To her, we owe special thanks. We also would like to thank Susan Woodruffe who acted as both Researcher and Administrator on the Voluntary Organizations Project. Her endeavours were exemplary as were her successes in maintaining contact between the Universities of Bradford and Warwick.

As with some of our earlier works, we were predisposed to using multiple methods to study the organizations in our sample. In this study, we have employed case studies, structured data from interviews, and used documentary and archival data wherever possible. Thus we hope that the reader interested in the more statistical representation of voluntary sector activities will find our research results equally stimulating and food for thought as the reader interested in our qualitative analyses. We also believe that multiple methods help our understanding in this field of research which has until now largely been absent from the analytical vocabulary of organizational analysis.

The research has been greatly helped along the way by a large number of people and institutions. We would of course like to thank the Leverhulme Trust for having the foresight to fund a great part of this project and we hope that the publication of this book is fitting reward for their confidence in us. Along the way we were guided by an Advisory Committee on which sat both academics and senior practitioners in charity management. To Sir Leslie Kirkley (a Senior Director in a number of charities, including Oxfam and War on Want), Andrew Dunsire (Professor of Politics at the University of York), and Ray Kipling (Deputy Director of the Royal National Lifeboat Institution) we owe our thanks. We also thank Dr John Sharp of the University of Bradford Management Centre who gave statistical advice, and Professor Andrew Pettigrew, Dr Richard Whipp, and Dr Robert Rosenfeld of the University of Warwick Business School who provided constructive criticism and helpful comments on the qualitative analyses.

Respondents in the sample organizations gave their time and information freely and showed great interest in the research project. In particular, the organizations which enabled us to conduct case studies were extremely helpful and our special thanks must go to all staff in St Dunstan's, RNLI, RNIB, Oxfam, and Christian Aid. We hope that all participants in the study will enjoy reading our interpretation of their context and that the findings will be of use to practitioners in the field of charity management as they face the challenges and opportunities of the nineteen nineties.

Richard J. Butler,
David C. Wilson,
University of Warwick,
June 1989

Chapter one

An introduction to charities: what are they and how do they operate?

This book is about how charities work. From the perspective of organization theory (and by most definitions) a charity is a distinct and unusual form of organization. Why should millions of people in the Western world give money and gifts to charities? Donors never see their money again. They get apparently nothing in return, and in some cases most of the funds are used in a different country to support starving people in the Third World, for example. One answer is that human rationality can and often does embrace the concept of *giving* for moral, religious, or other motives. Altruism is a fundamental part of human rationality and altruistic behaviour is the foundation stone of very many charities in Britain and elsewhere in the world. Without unselfish regard for others, there would be no place for charitable organizations in our society.

Altruism accounts for one important stimulus to charitable activity and the spirit of self-help dominates much of the rest. As Smiles (1898) notes, man soon loses faith in systems and procedures which are guided and ruled by legislation. Man can often see no connection between his actions and the actions of organized institutions. Help from 'without' often enfeebles mankind, but self-help or help from 'within' encourages learning and invigorates (Smiles 1898: Chapter 1). The activities of most self-help groups are founded upon these principles and whilst these organizations are not legally classified as charities in Britain, their ethos permeates much of the concept and practice of charitable giving and charitable organization.

This book is the result of a study of a number of charities in Britain. The study concentrated upon how some of the large and increasing number of charities in Britain were managed. Charities in three areas of activity were examined, these being:

1. International agencies (including religiously based charities).
2. Charities dealing with the visually handicapped.
3. Charities performing sea-rescue.

How did these organizations decide to allocate gifts of money to particular projects? How did the managers of these organizations recognize that the time had come for a change in the level or the area of activities? Did such organizations develop along the lines of a consciously formulated strategy, or did they muddle through, tackling problems one at a time in a piecemeal fashion? How was the organization itself organized? Was the design of the organization a help or a hindrance to its activities? Did the charity appear to be efficient in using and allocating resources? All these and other questions were the stimulus for this book.

Before we embark upon the details and the findings of the study, it is first of all necessary to examine some of the very special and possibly unique constraints and opportunities which face the managers of charities. It might be argued that management is pretty much the same in its fundamentals in any kind of organization. But that is not wholly the case for the management of charities.

Whilst there *are* a number of similarities between the roles of chief executives in Shell or ICI and the directors of major charities such as Oxfam or the National Trust, the context in which they operate is, in many respects, dissimilar. This is true not only of the present context, but is also true of the genesis and the history of the charitable sector which bears a heavy hand on current strategies, developments, and management practice. We shall examine the major features of these contexts in the next sections.

The gift relationship

Managers of charities must take into account their role as 'brokers' alongside their other professional management activities. This is because the charity acts as an intermediary between givers (of money and other resources) and receivers of services (beneficiaries) who are often remote in time and in place (see Figure 1.1). This is the 'gift relationship' described by Marcel Mauss (1954) who looked at the concept of the gift in remote Polynesian societies, and elaborated by Richard Titmuss (1970) with respect to the voluntary giving of blood in Britain. During this study, 3,325 blood donors were asked the question: *Why did they first decide to become a blood donor?* The answers were then coded into the following categories:

1. Altruism (26.4 per cent of answers), e.g. a general desire to help people or society, or to help medical research especially for babies.
2. Response to appeals from the Blood Transfusion Service (18 per cent of answers).
3. Personal appeal, e.g. from a friend to give blood (13.2 per cent of answers).
4. Reciprocity, e.g. a repayment for a transfusion received in the past (9.8 per cent of answers).

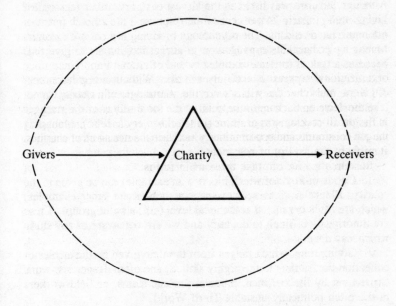

Figure 1.1 The gift relationship

5. Continuation, e.g. of people who started donating blood during World War 2 (6.7 per cent of answers).
6. Awareness of the need for blood, e.g. having witnessed an accident or a stay in hospital (not themselves needing blood) (6.4 per cent of answers).
7. Defence services, e.g. since 1945 a group in the military who experience pressure to donate blood. Often rewarded by 48-hour passes (5.0 per cent of answers).
8. Duty, e.g. through moral or other feelings of duty (3.5 per cent of answers).
9. To obtain a benefit, e.g. to discover blood group or a health check (1.8 per cent of answers).
10. Gratitude for good health, e.g. people who had experienced good health all their lives and viewed donating blood as a form of repayment (1.4 per cent of answers).
11. Donor belonged to a rare blood group, e.g. hence felt a particular responsibility to give blood (1.1 per cent of answers).
12. Miscellaneous (5 per cent of answers).

Although altruism was listed as the largest category, other reasons for giving blood (nearly 74 per cent of the responses) are a hotch-potch of often unrelated reasons. The psychology of giving is a complex matter. Managing a charitable organization to attract individuals to give thus becomes a task of intricate complexity and of crucial importance since organizational survival is certainly at stake. Without a regular supply of givers, most charities will not survive. A manager of a charity cannot take the decision to change a supplier in the same way as can a manager in the profit-making corporate world (Hickson *et al.* 1986). Managing the gift relationship must take primacy in charities since all other activities stem from the receipt of resources.

Resource giving can take three main forms:

1. Goods-in-kind (of which blood is an example) can be given to the charity. Blankets, clothing, newspapers, bottles are other examples, which are often organized at the local level (e.g. a scout group). These are notoriously difficult to quantify and we are not aware of any study which has done so.

2. Giving time, which ranges from the time given by the armies of collection-box rattlers to the highly skilled, and often dangerous, work carried out by lifeboat men, mountain rescue teams, or field workers in the often politically unstable Third World.

3. Giving money; although this is still difficult to quantify precisely, it is much easier than the other two kinds of giving. Recent studies by the Charities Aid Foundation and the Institute of Fiscal Studies, London, assess the total amount of money given to British charity as around 5 per cent of the Gross National Product.

Saxon-Harrold *et al.* (1987) reveal that charitable giving in Britain per adult earning a weekly income of up to £80 is about £10 per week (at 1980 prices). Thereafter, giving money rises fairly steeply to a plateau of about £30 per week at a weekly income of £120. Plotting giving against age gives a V relationship with the lowest incidence of giving at the 40-year-old mark (approximately). Younger and older than this reflects increasing generosity. Presumably, the greater family and financial commitments of the 40-year-old head of household reflects the drop in charitable giving.

Our measure of the extent of charitable giving is taken from eight years of figures from the Charities Aid Foundation (CAF). This gives the total overall income and the total voluntary income of the top 200 charities classifies as 'Grant Seeking' by CAF.

Both total income and voluntary income of the top 200 charities has been rising on average by 30 per cent and 27 per cent respectively per year when the Gross National Product of the British Economy (GNP) has been rising at a lesser rate. In 1984, the voluntary income alone of the top 200 charities was 4 per cent of GNP.

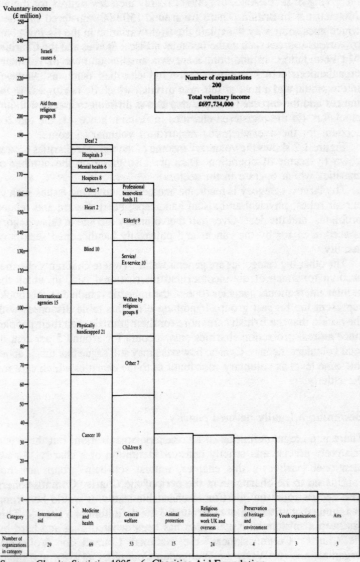

Voluntary income
(£ million)

					Number of organizations
					200
					Total voluntary income
					£697,734,000

| Israeli causes 6 |
| Aid from religious groups 8 |
| Deaf 2 |
| Hospitals 3 |
| Mental health 6 |
| Hospices 8 |
| Other 7 | Professional benevolent funds 11 |
| Heart 2 |
| | Elderly 9 |
| Blind 10 |
	Service/ Ex-service 10
International agencies 15		Welfare by religious groups 8
	Physically handicapped 21
		Other 7
	Cancer 10	Children 8

Category	International aid	Medicine and health	General welfare	Animal protection	Religious missionary work UK and overseas	Preservation of heritage and environment	Youth organizations	Arts
Number of organizations in category	29	69	53	15	24	4	3	3

Source: Charity Statistics 1985 – 6, Charities Aid Foundation

Figure 1.2 Voluntary income of the major sectors (the top 200 charities)

The figure will certainly be an underestimate of the proportion of wealth given by the British people, since it excludes giving in kind and the giving of time. Also, of course, it only includes figures for the top 200 charities in Britain. There are around 150,000 registered charities, which goes some way to explain the slight variation in the figures given by various sources such as the Institute of Fiscal Studies and the Charities Aid Foundation. In addition, there is a smaller number of voluntary organizations which are non-registered charities (such as Amnesty International and a host of self-help groups) which do not appear in the figures and the income for these charities is difficult to assess with any precision. Of the registered charities in Britain, however, the top 200 account for the overwhelming majority of voluntary income.

Figure 1.2 shows the voluntary income of the top 200 charities broken down by sector of operation. Data are also given on the number of charities which operate in the sectors.

The largest category is medicine and health, covering issues such as cancer relief, physical and visual handicaps, heart disease and related problems, and the deaf. Over half the voluntary income in this category is accounted for by the cancer and physically handicapped sectors of activity.

The other big categories are general welfare (where children's charities account for much of the income) and International Aid, in which the secular international agencies (one of the industries studied in this book) represent the biggest group. If nothing else, this table dispenses with the notion that the British care more for their animals than their people, since animal protection charities only account for around 5 per cent of total voluntary income. Cynics, however, may still argue that this is about the same level as voluntary contributions to the charities which care for the elderly.

Becoming a legally defined charity

There is no legal definition of a voluntary organization, but there is a relatively precise and strictly enforced definition of a charity. As we mentioned earlier in this chapter, mutual self-help groups are not considered to be charitable in the eyes of the Charity Commissioners who decide upon the question of charitable status. It would be wrong to assume that no ambiguity surrounded the definition of a charity. This has been a substantial issue which has been debated long and hard by the Charity Commissioners, the National Council for Voluntary Organizations (NCVO), the Wolfenden Committee (1978), and many others. Precise legal details can be found in Chesterman (1979) and Gladstone (1982).

It is sufficient for our purposes here to note that becoming registered as a charity endows sizeable fiscal benefits to the organizations. These take the form of various tax concessions which are thus made available. Although the Inland Revenue does not automatically concede tax advantages to legally registered charities, more than 90 per cent of currently registered charities enjoy exemption from income and corporation taxes. As Chesterman (1979) notes, charity law can be quite accurately described as little other than a sub-set of tax laws with little concern for anything else. To reinforce this point, the range of fiscal liabilities from which registered charities are exempt has grown progressively wider in recent years and the real value of exemptions has increased as the taxes levied upon non-charitable organizations has increased. The levels of capital gains tax and corporation tax have increased substantially over the last fifteen years or so, as have the taxes levied on those who donate or bequeath monies to organizations which are not registered charities.

Becoming a legally registered charity also means that the organization can set up an independent trading company which is exempt from a similar range of tax liabilities providing that trading profits are directed solely toward support of the original, primary charitable purpose of the organization. Well-known trading companies of registered charities include Oxfam's retail outlets, mail order and greeting card operations, the National Society for the Prevention of Cruelty to Children's mail order and card service, and the Royal National Lifeboat Institution's trading company which runs souvenir, gift, and Christmas card sales.

The laws of charitable trusts are an important division of the law of Equity. They are complex and ancient laws. Some are based, for example, on the transfer of property to descendants (*Quia Emptores*, 1290) or to the Church (*Mortmain Statutes*, 1300–1391). Three Acts also underpin the law of charitable trusts. The Charitable Uses Act of 1601 provides a framework for the gradual evolution of the legal meaning of charity. The Charitable Trusts Act of 1853 was a fine tuning of the previous Act, whilst the Charities Act of 1960 was definitive in requiring the introduction of a register of charitable organizations and in introducing the compulsory registration of charities.

There are four essential pillars of what is, in law, considered a charitable activity: education, relief of the poor, the advancement of religion, and other services which are considered in general to be beneficial to the community. The trustees of the organization must not benefit in any way from the organization and the beneficiaries cannot be those who give (hence the reason that self-help groups are excluded).

There must be some indication of 'public good' in the services offered (i.e. a number of people could benefit, not just a select few) and the organization must not be political or ideological, or both. This means that political parties or trade unions cannot be registered charities. Neither can most professional associations since they exist to benefit their members (although there are exceptions as we shall see) and pressure groups cannot be charities if their aim is interpreted as trying to effect changes in the law.

There is currently growing concern over the implications of these laws as being too restrictive and as being in the interests of the Charity Commissioners and others at the expense of organizational flexibility and change (Wilson 1984). There is also criticism that the law is not up to handling the range of current problems and issues which face modern voluntary organizations. For example, an organization such as Oxfam, which is a registered charity, may *relieve* suffering in all parts of the world. This activity is considered charitable and finds its roots in religiously based nineteenth century social philosophy. However, an organization which pressures for *changes* in what are considered to be the causes of poverty and suffering would be refused charitable status. Current management in Oxfam recognizes that strategic development of the organization must to some extent be aimed at attacking and addressing the issues of cause rather than be wholly a reactive charity to disaster when it strikes. Yet this is likely to bring the organization into conflict with the Charity Commissioners who would deem such activities to be uncharitable in their terms.

Similarly, the rather dated and rigid charity laws have brought organizations such as the Amnesty International Trust into conflict with the Charity Commissioners. Amnesty International is not legally a charity. Charitable status was refused in 1978 and again in 1981 when Mr Justice Slade argued that two of the organization's objectives were political and could only be achieved by changes in the law or the administration of the countries in question. These two objectives were:

1. The release of prisoners of conscience.
2. To procure the abolition of torture or other degrading treatment.

The report of the Charity Commission (1981), which was aimed at modernizing and relaxing some of the rather rigid definitions of charity outlined above, has only served to confuse and make matters worse in many respects. For example, a voluntary organization may now become a charity even if it engages in some persuasion and is committed to a particular ideology or set of beliefs. Child Poverty Action Group is one such organization which is a legally registered charity. Charities such as these may help the Government to reach a decision on social policy by providing arguments and ideological perspectives. However, charities must not attempt to pressure Government to follow a specific course of action by means of the same arguments and ideologies! To do this would be to ensure the demise of charitable status.

Some of the relaxations of charity law are evident in the field of intermediary bodies such as the Council for Voluntary Youth Services or the Charity Information Bureaux which operate alongside statutory services. Previously denied charitable status, virtually all these organizations have now been deemed to be charitable by the Charity Commissioners (National Council for Voluntary Organizations 1983).

Managers of voluntary organizations which are seeking charitable status are therefore open to the possibility of disguising the true purpose of the organization in order to gain charitable status. Once given, charitable status is rarely taken away. The Charity Commissioners do not have the resources necessary to police the charitable sector overall. The Commissioners are helped in this regard by the Inland Revenue, but both organizations are so busy with a growing work load in the charitable sector, that subsequent transgressions by organizations often go unnoticed.

The organizations we discuss in this book are all registered charities. One reason for this is that comparison between organizations is made possible and meaningful. The differences between non-charities and charities are sufficient to render comparisons extremely difficult since their legal status, their operating context, and the issues with which they deal are mostly very different. As Saxon-Harrold (1986) has argued, charitable status has an impact upon the internal management and strategy of voluntary organizations. We have therefore controlled for this by including only registered charities in our sample.

Another reason for choosing registered charities is that data are much more readily available for them. This is particularly true of archival, financial, and strategy data which for non-registered charities can be scrappy or unreliable (or both) and occasionally are non-existent. Since the present study involved developing strategic profiles for our sample organizations for which the data were sourced from multiple methods, the greater the availability of data the better.

Charities in context

If we are to understand the present structure and strategies of charities, we would be wise to pay heed to the infamous Irishman who, when asked for directions by a stranger, replied, 'I wouldn't start from here if I were you'. In just the same way, it would be folly to embark upon a description and an analysis of current charitable activities without reference to the substantial influences of the past in which the kind of voluntary activity we often take for granted today was created often through strife and struggle.

Our intention here is not to give a full account of such developments. This is beyond the scope of the present book. Nevertheless, it is necessary to place the organizations with which we deal in their appropriate historical context. The present chapter deals very generally with the development of the voluntary movement in Britain. In later chapters, the reader will find detailed histories of particular organizations, which we felt were representative of particular policies or reflected typical tensions and changes, and further historical data will be found here in relation to the emergence of specific areas of activity, e.g. the welfare of the visually handicapped.

Charity: one of three ways of allocating resources and of providing services

As Butler (1983) has suggested, the present-day mixed economy can be divided into three broad areas. These are *the market*, which consists of commercial organizations which survive for the most part through the generation of surplus value; *the statutory sector*, which includes central and local government agencies; and *the voluntary sector*, which includes registered charities and non-registered charities, such as pressure groups and self-help organizations.

Markets allocate resources by means of price which provides a signal to entrepreneurs and capitalists to move into activities promising greater profits and out of areas where profits are diminishing. This system only works efficiently under conditions of sufficient competition, but can still give rise to a number of externalities which penalize non-participants in a particular market (for instance, through a factory which produces air pollution from its manufacturing processes and is penalized for this). Furthermore, individuals can be excluded from markets due to lack of income or other barriers to entry.

If price is the first method of resource allocation, then the second is central planning. Throughout the twentieth century, governments have utilized planning mechanisms, in the first place to direct the economies in the World Wars, and then, learning from these experiences, to direct resources during peacetime through certain manufacturing industries and social, health, and educational services. The assumption behind these plans had been that they have covered particular vital strategic resources, such as shipbuilding, or services which are considered central and vital to populations, such as health.

Whereas the specifics of planning may vary tremendously from case to case, there is always one common element. A higher authority makes decisions about what is needed by whom and in what quantity. Pseudo-prices may be used, as in the nationalized railways, to reduce the level of subsidy required and to provide an illusion of market mechanisms, but these prices are of necessity ultimately set by political dictate.

It is not the purpose of this book to draw conclusions about the worthiness of either of these two systems. We can note, however, that there are arguments across a range of industrialized countries that planning of manufacturing industries has led to a number of unfortunate consequences, particularly lower efficiency and rigidity in the face of technical change. Increasingly, we can expect governments to look towards non-planning methods for resource allocation, although it is acknowledged that when it comes to the 'softer' products such as health care, education, and welfare, there are considerable problems in relying solely on the marketplace for service provision since it relies so heavily on profitable returns.

It is for these reasons that charity, the third way of allocating resources, is becoming increasingly emphasized and is expanding to take an important position in the national economy. From the perspective of government, this is an attractive development. If the voluntary sector can take over some of the activities previously provided by the state, then this allows scope for state spending in other areas, or allows reductions in the overall level of spending and the setting up of politically popular tax culling programmes. It also creates greater flexibility (in theory) for state agencies, which have been traditionally inflexible in the face of changing political or technical demands. From the point of view of the public, charity provides an expressive outlet where people can choose to support causes special to them. This is likely to be viewed more favourably than support which is gained through the tax system for example. Decisions to support charities are, of course, made in very different ways to either market place or planned economies. It is here that the 'gift relationship' described earlier in this chapter explains many of the motives behind individual support of charities.

Today's economy sees a wide spread of service provision by both the statutory and voluntary sectors. For example, child care services are provided by both state agencies, through the Department of Health and Social Security, and by voluntary organizations such as Barnardos, the National Society for the Prevention of Cruelty to Children, or the National Children's Home. There is often considerable overlap and co-operation in the provision of services between the voluntary and the statutory sectors. This is also true of social and medical welfare organizations.

Whilst there is less overlap and virtually no co-operation between the voluntary sector and commercial enterprises, except perhaps for certain inner city refurbishment schemes and some housing developments, the partnership between voluntary and statutory organizations has a long history. It has not always been a smooth or an amicable relationship as Leat *et al*. (1981) illustrate. At the very least, collaboration dates back to Elizabethan times.

The history and development of charities

Charity law began in effect in 1601 with the Statute of Charitable Uses

Act. In tandem with the Poor Law (or as it was then termed the Statute of Poor Relief), statutory and charitable provisions of services went hand in hand. Statutory agencies were to be formally responsible for attending to the needs of the poor, whilst charitable organizations were to accept responsibility for virtually every other social ill! In fact, the range of problems attended to by charities at this time was very wide indeed. It included not only the welfare of persons (the aged or orphans, for example) but also the repair of natural disasters to objects such as roads, bridges, riverbanks, and sea walls. One quite natural result of this was that charity in general became so wide-ranging its precise definition became impossible.

Given that *laissez-faire* was the popular and accepted role of the government, charity continued to be spread across a vast range of services and activities up until the nineteenth century. It took the vigorous and seemingly tireless contributions of individuals who reacted to *laissez-faire* indifference coupled with nation-wide epidemics such as the massive outbreak of cholera in the 1840s to sharpen the responsibilities of the state and so define the domain of charitable activity. Of course, the events of social history and policy during the nineteenth century were far more complex than can be described here, but some important events took place which were to have implications for charities which still persist today.

The conditions of the poor became much more widely known through the writings of influential men such as Owen and Cobbett. Equally, the popular didactic novels of the 1840s (for example, by Dickens or Kingsley) brought the plight of the poor and the insidious effects of increasing industrialization to the attention of many more people than at any time previously (Tillotson 1954, Rooff 1957).

The church also began to take an active and what was to be a fundamental role in charitable work. Prior to the nineteenth century, the Church had remained supremely distant from the social issues of the poor and the needy. It was a fragmented organization with no one clear voice other than the strains of the evangelical sub-set which could be heard debating the existentialist concerns of the other world. Earthly concerns were not in their portfolio. Yet, the nineteenth century saw the Church gradually become engaged in the activities of existing charities and then to go on to found a great number of new charitable organizations. As Rooff (1957: 9) notes: 'The majority of the voluntary societies founded in the nineteenth century had a religious basis, while much social legislation was carried through in response to religious conviction or humanitarian principles.'

We shall see that the Church dominates the foundation of a great number of the organizations in our sample. In particular, welfare for the blind and the relief of poverty and distress are inextricably rooted in religious foundations and the moral and philosophical overtones of this genesis should not be forgotten in any analysis of charitable activity.

Many of the churches also set about organizing moral welfare activities. Indeed, at the outset of welfare for the blind, the Church was more interested in reading the scriptures to the visually handicapped than in helping them integrate better into society! Some well-known voluntary organizations were founded at this time and were to carry through the message of religiously based moral welfare to the present day. The Salvation Army (founded in 1865 by William Booth) is an example of this as is Barnardos which was founded upon strong religious principles. Less well-known organizations, such as the Bible Lands Society, demonstrate that concerned Christianity spread outside the shores of Great Britain. This organization was founded in 1854 in Turkey, which was one of the original Bible lands, and had Lord Shaftesbury, a strong-minded Protestant, as a patron.

Other churches such as the Roman and the Anglican also began to found and to encourage charitable activities rooted in the furtherance of moral welfare. The Quakers were also notably successful in achieving progress in charitable organizations. Notable here is the work of Elizabeth Fry but the vast number of schools and other educational establishments which emerged under the Quakers' banner is testament to the energy and zeal of the Quaker movement.

Rooff (1957) also outlines how the principles of modern case work concerning social issues such as those practised by NSPCC are rooted in the emergence of the Jewish Board of Guardians which was set up to give assistance to needy families and to investigate and assist the Jewish immigrants who were settling in a new country.

If the religious basis of many charities is one dominant influence upon their philosophies and their operations, the other dominant influences come from the gradually greater definition and responsibilities of the statutory services and the emergence of the Welfare State which occurred throughout the early and middle twentieth century to the present.

The statutory provision of social services

Until the adoption of the Beveridge report by the Labour Government of 1945–51, charities acted as providers of major services such as care of children, care of the elderly, care of the handicapped, and running many hospitals. The Beveridge Report (1942) recommended the large-scale provision of services in these and other areas by statutory bodies. Comprehensive statutory services finally sealed the demise of the Poor Law and the state was obliged to provide basic social services to every resident. The implications of this for charities were far reaching. It shaped the current context of charitable activities.

Whilst according to Wolfenden (1978) the voluntary sector seemed to 'mark time' for some years after the Second World War, from the 1950s onward, great developments and new areas of activity took place in the voluntary sector. Summarizing from the report of the Wolfenden Committee (p. 20):

1. An increase in the provision of specialist services by voluntary organizations. These services were those not available from statutory sources. ·
2. The rapid growth of pressure groups.
3. The rapid growth of mutual-help groups such as the Pre-School Playgroups Association.
4. The growth of the number of co-ordinating bodies at the national and local levels.
5. The increasing encouragement of voluntary activity generally by local and central government and the total or partial funding thereof.

The result of this explosion of voluntary activities on the one hand, more precise definitions of the role of the state and the increasing inter-dependence between state agencies and the voluntary sector on the other, has been the focus of a number of fundamental debates concerning largely the role and the autonomy of voluntary organizations in the political economy. We outline some of these issues next.

The current context of charitable organizations

From the emergence of the welfare state and the parallel expansion of the voluntary sector, comes an increasing and current need for both statutory and voluntary organizations to be aware of each other's activities and, often, to co-operate on particular projects or areas of activity. Quite naturally, debates on social policy have emerged. Which services should be provided as a statutory right to clients and which services should voluntary organizations provide? To what extent should clients have the choice to receive services for a particular need from both statutory and voluntary organizations? Since history rarely gives us neat packages of development in economies, the inter-relationships between voluntary and statutory organizations emerge as a complex and tightly interwoven web of pluralist provision of services.

The statutory/voluntary relationship

The 1970s and the early 1980s presented a fairly optimistic picture of voluntary and statutory organizations working side by side. There were exceptions, of course, as Leat *et al.* (1981) point out. In particular, the funding of voluntary organizations by statutory bodies was argued to erode strategic autonomy and inhibit the flexibility of voluntary organizations (one of their treasured assets). In a previous work, we also recognized that:

> In particular, [voluntary] strategy is constrained when money is received from state agencies which, justifiably from their perspective, wish to see their financial support utilized in a manner congruent with their interests and which do not always coincide with the preferences of the voluntary organization.
>
> (Wilson and Butler 1986: 526)

In the language of organization theory, the above can be described as a dependence relationship (Emerson 1962, Thompson 1967). Where such dependencies are created (through the finance relationship for example) then imbalances in power between the organizations necessarily is the result. As Saxon-Harrold (1986) noted, voluntary organizations which received funding from the government were obliged, often contractually, to co-operate with the wishes of the funding body. As the proportion of government funding grew bigger (as a proportion of total income) then the more the power balance shifted toward the funder.

The early research which went into the compilation of this book again reinforced the potency of the funding relationship as eroding strategic autonomy. Our initial investigations into organizations such as Oxfam, Metropolitan Community Transport Schemes (MCT), and NSPCC, for example, revealed the varying strength of the dependence relationship.

Oxfam receives very little money from statutory sources. Over the last four or so years, government grants have only been between 7 per cent and 8 per cent of total income. Yet, receipt of a government grant means that Oxfam often has to operate along the lines suggested by government which are not always those favoured by Oxfam. Sometimes such constraints also seem to fly in the face of common sense.

In one joint venture between Oxfam and the Overseas Development Agency of central government, Oxfam was pressured to make what turned out to be, at the least, an uneconomic decision. The pressure was for Oxfam to buy British rather than Japanese and purchase only Land-Rover vehicles for a particular overseas project. Not only were Land-Rovers more expensive than their Japanese manufactured counterparts, but also there was no provision for their service or for spare parts, yet these were available for the Japanese vehicles. So, once a Land-Rover suffered a breakdown, its repair proved expensive and occasionally impossible.

Of course, beyond this small percentage of statutory funding and its associated influence, Oxfam is strategically a free agent for the most part. This is not true of the Metropolitan Community Transport (MCT) voluntary organizations. Here, 90 per cent of the income of these

15

organizations came from statutory sources. Closely linked to government agencies through Councils for Voluntary Services, which are run by local authorities, voluntary transport schemes are not in a position to make decisions about where and when they should operate or whom their clients should be without first consulting the funding statutory body. Indeed, in the MCT organization reported in Wilson and Butler (1986), the majority of clients for the transport scheme were local government departments!

Voluntary organizations which receive government funding, but can themselves determine its extent, have a far greater range of strategic discretion and autonomy. The National Society for the Prevention of Cruelty to Children (NSPCC) is an example of this. NSPCC does receive some funding from statutory agencies and largely this is mediated through local government for specific projects. Often, this means that statutory Social Service departments and NSPCC work together on the same case or the same set of cases. Here, the way in which the cases are handled is largely determined by the local authority (i.e. the funding body) and this is sometimes at odds with the ways in which NSPCC would otherwise have handled the case. According to Parton (1981: 392), NSPCC sees 'removal of a child from its parents . . . as a first rather than a last resort' with the prosecution of the parents following close behind (NSPCC is one of very few organizations in Britain to have the power to bring about prosecutions). State agencies generally prefer to work with the family largely on a case-by-case basis and retain the child within the home and the family if this is possible.

Over the last ten years, the percentage of NSPCC's total income from statutory sources has been steadily getting smaller. In 1977, total government support of the organization was around 25 per cent. In 1986–7 this has dropped to around 5 per cent. It is at the discretion of NSPCC's managers whether or not this level of funding should increase or decrease. During the organization's centenary year and thereafter, NSPCC fund raisers have been looking to use corporate income rather than government money which perhaps indicates an unwillingness to get too closely tied in to governmental social policies on child welfare.

A voluntary organization which can choose the level of government financial support is far less dependent and far less subject to possible constraints on its autonomy than those organizations which rely upon substantial government funding. Furthermore, an organization which can find alternative sources of funding to statutory sources is even better placed to reduce its dependence (Hickson *et al.* 1971).

This has implications for the strategy of all voluntary organizations towards givers and we shall explore this in detail in later chapters. At this point it serves to emphasize the urgent need for the managers of voluntary organizations to invest substantial time and energy into managing the funding relationship.

The political economy of the voluntary sector

The funding relationship is not the whole story of the interrelationships between voluntary organizations and the economy at large. We have seen already that decisional autonomy is eroded from the managers of those organizations which apply to become legally registered charities. They can only pursue certain specified goals in certain specified ways.

A further factor must be taken into consideration when examining the context of current voluntary activity. Wilson and Butler (1985) have characterized the political economy of state/voluntary sector relations as resembling a neo-corporatist framework (Figure 1.3). That is, direct control in a legislative and operational sense has been devolved from central government to large associations (the most well known of these is the National Council for Voluntary Organizations, NCVO). These associations act as private agents of public policy (see Lehmbruch 1977, 1982, and Streeck and Schmitter 1984). Associations can administer terms of behaviour for their member organizations — membership is not mandatory. In this respect, private associations act both as policy implementers and as policy formulators for their constituents. Such constituencies can be, for example, health care, the care and re-settlement of offenders, mental health welfare, or the care of the visually handicapped.

At the time of writing, self regulation through the associations seems to be working quite well, although no association has yet managed to negotiate with the state over the terms of eligibility for charitable status. Moves toward this are in evidence. Recently NCVO has undertaken a programme of action to advise its constituent voluntary organizations which are seeking charitable status. This takes the form of building up a collection of cases which it is hoped will eventually act as legal precedents for applications (NCVO 1984). If this is successful, then policy control over charitable status will be effectively devolved from the state to the associations which will be empowered to make decisions on behalf of the state.

As Wilson and Butler (1985) note, central government is still currently perceived to have a great deal of influence over strategic decision making. It was reported by managers in seventy-two of seventy-five voluntary organizations studied, that government departments were extremely influential in constraining and restraining strategic behaviour and direction.

The current structure of state and voluntary relations can be seen as an outcome of the process by which the state legitimizes certain areas of voluntary activity. This legitimacy is not just confined to rather rigid analyses of corporatism and the devolution of political authority. In order to be considered in any way legitimate, voluntary organizations must

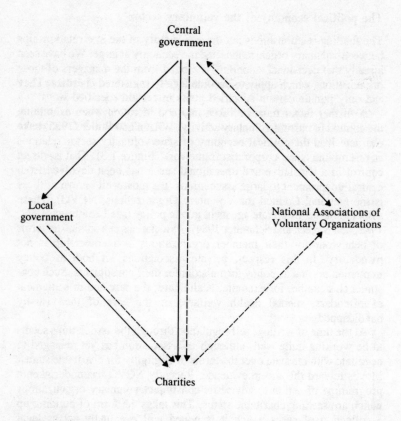

Central
government

Local
government

National Associations of
Voluntary Organizations

Charities

Legend

⟶ Funding relationships
- - -▶ Mediation and negotiation of interests

Figure 1.3 The neo-corporatist framework

either add to, reinforce, or fill gaps in currently provided state services. Above all, co-operation with existing state services is viewed as critical by central government agencies, such as the Voluntary Services Unit in the Home Office.

Such co-operation can, it seems, take many forms but the message for voluntary sector managers is clear. Align your organization with the *modus operandi* of the state otherwise pressure to change or rejection of recognition as a charity will be the results. This message comes through loud and clear from our own research and the studies of others in the voluntary sector who are concerned with state/voluntary sector alignments (see, for example, Aves 1969, Fitzgerald *et al.* 1977, Johnson 1981 and Moyer 1983). All of these authors argue with respect to a number of areas of voluntary activity that life is very hard for organizations which the state does not see as legitimate. It looks as if a number of propositions could be made as to what is considered legitimate if we synthesize much of the work described above:

1. The state grants autonomy to one voluntary organization for the provision of a specific service. Government departments do not themselves provide an equivalent service. The Royal National Lifeboat Institution (RNLI) is an example of this. Here, a voluntary organization is doing the job of what otherwise would be the task of a state agency, or possibly a number of private commercial concerns.
2. The state recognizes a small number of voluntary organizations to provide a specific service which is not provided by government departments. The Women's Royal Voluntary Service is an example of this with its meals on wheels services in hospitals. WRVS is also wholly funded by the Home Office.
3. The state acts as 2 above, but also provides similar and equivalent services through government departments. Oxfam and Save the Children Fund are examples, which often work alongside government relief agencies, such as Overseas Development Agency.
4. The state allows an undesignated number of voluntary organizations to operate and provide a general service in particular areas such as housing or child care. Government departments also provide a similar service. Examples of voluntary organizations in this category are NSPCC, Housing Associations, etc.

In all of these four categories, the state encourages voluntary activity to take place. The categories are not absolutely watertight conceptually and nor is this necessary. The point to be made is that in all the above cases, the state can utilize or benefit from the activities in the voluntary sector. Either the state does not have to provide the service at all, as is the case with RNLI, or gaps in the provision of statutory services are filled by voluntary activity, as in international relief agencies and housing associations. In the following two categories, the state/voluntary juxtaposition is less benevolently disposed:

5. The state remains neutral to the emergence of voluntary activity. There is neither encouragement nor active discouragement. Government departments usually provide a similar service, but this is not

always the case. Some self-help groups such as Alcoholics Anonymous are examples as well as some medical and social welfare organizations.

6.   The state discourages voluntary activity in particular areas of activity. Nor do government departments provide a similar service. Radical pressure groups, single issue groups, and politically ideological groups are examples.

The impact both of history and of the economy in which voluntary organizations operate must be taken into account when we begin to examine the ways in which these organizations are managed over time and in which ways they choose to embark upon particular strategies. We approach the concept of strategy and its pertinence to the voluntary sector in the next chapter.

Until now, we have been using the term voluntary organization to describe our unit of study. This has been appropriate to put this large sector of organized activities in their context. Hereafter, we shall be concentrating upon a sub-section of voluntary activities and looking solely at legally registered charities. For the reasons described earlier, this is in order to ensure comparability across the sample both in examining the strategic management of these organizations and the context in which their managers operate.

Chapter two

The domain of British charities

Charities are, for the large part, absent from the analytical vocabulary of both organization theory and strategic management. As Williamson and Ouchi (1981: 366) argue, charities are usually dismissed as slightly obscure organizations which defy systematic analysis and which do not lend themselves easily to the techniques and measurements of organizational analysis. We agree with the latter statement, but not the former. Charities in Britain, and indeed around the world, are no longer obscure. They are in the forefront of public, political, and corporate awareness. Recent campaigns such as 'Band Aid' or 'Comic Relief' cannot fail to be noticed by most people who own a television set, listen to the radio, or buy a newspaper.

The Band Aid Trust which was set up to receive donations had a total income of £69 million (source: Charity Statistics 1985–6). In the same year Oxfam received nearly £60 million, the National Trust received £70 million, and Save the Children Fund nearly £43 million. Total income for Britain's top 200 charities was virtually £300 million in 1985–6 and this figure does not include the many self-help groups, pressure groups, and campaigning organizations which are not classified legally as charities. Charities are big business. Yet when we look for evidence of the ways in which such organizations are managed and manage themselves in relation to their environments, evidence is extremely sketchy. There are isolated studies of particular aspects of intra-organizational aspects, such as the degree of bureaucratic or formal structure and studies of who gives to charities (and how much), but very little is known about the management of such organizations, how strategies are shaped and formulated, and how processes of organizational design, change, and adaptation take place.

Organizational structure

Ever since Chandler's (1963) study of the relationships between strategy and structure in organizations, researchers have been at pains to modify,

21

qualify, and generally extend this large field of enquiry (see, for example, Channon 1973). Despite their different approaches and their analytical perspectives, all agree on the fundamental importance of *both* structure and strategy in the management process. Managers must attend to both aspects when delineating the future direction of their organizations. Chandler (1963) argues a convincing case for the appropriateness of particular structural forms of organization which match, and thus make the most of, particular strategic initiatives. Other researchers have been more cautious in arguing such a link, but all give primacy to the element of structure as a constraint or an oppportunity to the strategy and the ultimate success of the enterprise.

The multi-million pound industries of the charitable sector therefore must bear examination from the structural point of view. It might be the case that the success of some organizations and the demise of others is to a large extent due to the structural configuration they adopt. In Chandler's terms, those who have in some way appropriately matched strategy and structure are thus likely to be the growing, thriving enterprises.

The present study aims to throw some light upon this question and to what extent it might be of relevance to the managers of charities. This is a question made even more burning since the advent of the works by authors such as Peters and Waterman (1982) and Kanter (1983) who argue that excellence in organizational performance is at least partially achieved through adopting particular structural forms. These authors give evidence from some of the most successful firms in North America that the successful companies share a structure which allows both flexibility and autonomy to both managers and employees, but which also is well-defined enough to ensure efficient delimitation of rules and administrative procedures. Such organizations are a combination (in the one firm) of both 'loose' and 'tight' structures.

Whilst the questions of organizational structure have had a long and influential history of research in both the public and the private commercial sectors, when the current authors turned to what had been done in the charitable sector, we found almost no work at all. Certainly, no systematic study of organizational structure had been attempted.

There is, however, a large literature on the structure and the functioning of communes and collective organizations generally (see, for example, Kanter's earlier and prolific work in this area, 1972, and Rothschild-Whitt 1979). The structures of work co-operatives and kibbutzim have also been fairly extensively covered (see, for example, Bradley and Gelb 1982 concerning the Mondragon co-operative in Spain, and Eccles 1981, Leviathan 1984 and Wilson and Rosenfeld 1989 on co-operative forms of organization). These studies are a good point of departure, but they are really too general to be applied to the specific contexts of British charities.

Turning specifically to the organizational structure of charities reveals an almost total gap in our research knowledge.

There are some exceptions, but these are rare and isolated studies. For example, Tsouderos (1955) and Chapin and Tsouderos (1956) examined the levels of formalization and bureaucratization in ten North American voluntary organizations. Using time series analysis, they argued that there appeared to be a tendency for newly established and initially informally structured voluntary organizations to progress toward the institutionalization of their structures to become formal bureaucracies. As far as we are aware, no further large-scale study of this kind has ever emerged on either side of the Atlantic, although many authors have alluded to the bureaucratization process (e.g. Meyer 1983, Scott 1982, Brooke 1984).

Yet if formalization is a 'natural' progression for charities as they develop, there are some fundamental implications for their management. We know, for example, that bureaucratic organizations are slow to adapt to change, rarely innovate, are inflexible, and often display a number of other inbuilt dysfunctions (Blau and Scott 1962, Merton 1957). If charities develop this institutional hardening of their arteries, they will lose some of their flexibility and adaptability, two of their most prized and arguably distinguishing features.

This book is an attempt to throw some light upon these and related issues in the strategic management of British charities. Our early work in compiling data for this book and the research of others who have tangentially thrown light upon the question of organizational structure in charities (for example, Brooke (1984) and Saxon-Harrold (1986)), led us to believe that whilst a variety of organizational forms are possible choices, three common structural forms account for the majority of organizations in the charitable sector. We discuss these in the following section.

Some common structures for charities

The choices facing managers in the charitable sector are both complex and far reaching when considering organizational structure. They can choose a purely functional structure in which tasks are differentiated into separate identifiable departments or sections in the one organization. These are often arranged in some sort of hierarchy with communication flows from the various sub-divisions to the managerial and executive apex. Organizations such as the Royal Commonwealth Society for the Blind and the Red Cross are examples of this type of structure (see Figures 2.1a and 2.1b).

Other common structures are the divisional and the matrix (or project) arrangements of activities. The divisional structure allows for distinct

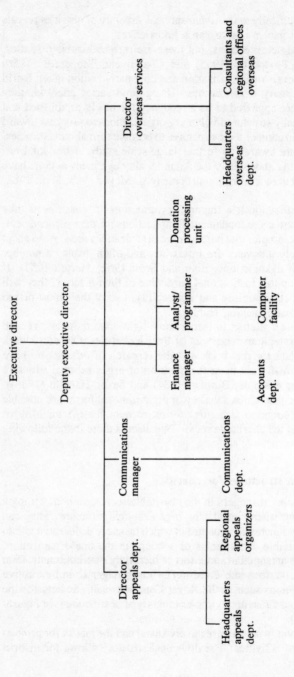

Figure 2.1a Organizational structure: Royal Commonwealth Society for the Blind, a functional structure

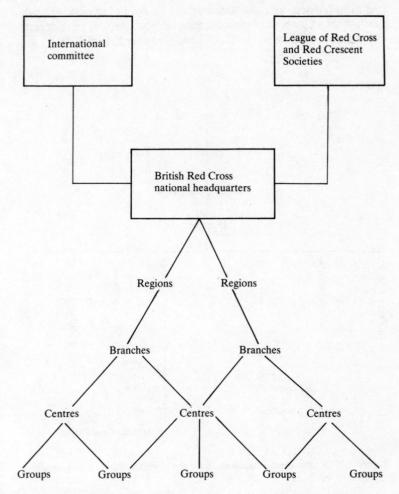

Figure 2.1b Organizational structure: Red Cross, a functional structure

branches of organizational activities to function simultaneously. For example, Save the Children Fund (STCF) is divisionalized into home-based activities and the provision of services overseas. The home-based division has a number of regional branches further broken down into groups in towns and cities. These groups have a fund-raising role but, as STCF operates in the UK as well as overseas, they can also act as operational units. The other branch of STCF covers the areas of overseas operations (Africa, Asia, the Americas and the Pacific regions). At head-quarters are a number of functional departments. Heads of these departments report directly to the Chief Executive (see Figure 2.2).

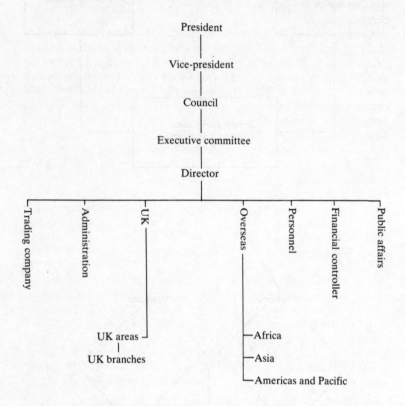

Figure 2.2 Organizational structure: Save the Children Fund, a divisionalized structure

As Chandler (1963) notes, divisionalized structures have certain advantages and operating problems which do not occur in the purely functional structure. Divisionalization facilitates growth and flexibility. Since divisions operate relatively autonomously, resources and energies can be channelled into those parts of the organization where they are needed the most. This can occur without affecting the other branch or branches of the organization. Conflicts can occur, however, where headquarters assumes not only a co-ordinating role, but also wants to retain policy control.

Tension arises between the operating divisions 'in the field' and central headquarters. Operational divisions assume that they have the appropriate knowledge to implement and modify policy decisions as local conditions require, whilst headquarters insists on its rather more distanced policies being followed.

Conflict can also occur between different divisions in the same branch of the organization, particularly where resources are scarce and demand from all the divisions exceeds supply. This is exemplified *in extremis* in the context of medical charities (see Deans 1989). There is the tension between offering a welfare service to relieve medical conditions and research work to find out the cause of maladies such as cancer, AIDS, and coronary diseases. The scarce resources, often exacerbated by funding from outside agencies, highlight this conflict since funders tend to pick only one of these two organizational objectives.

Matrix structures are just as rare in the charitable sector as they are in commercial and public organizations. In theory, at least, the matrix form would seem to be ideal for the operations of many charities. This is because the matrix form is organized around specific projects rather than around a fixed hierarchy or divisionalization. This structure is extremely flexible and adaptable in the face of change. Project teams, groups, and special working parties are formed in order to handle a particular project (for example, fund raising in 'new' areas, or developing existing services) and these teams can be abandoned or retained as circumstances dictate. Any formal hierarchy is put on one side during project membership and a project leader may be from any level in a functional hierarchy. There is at least a *prima facie* case for choosing a flexible structure such as the matrix for charities.

However, such structures have their own inbuilt problems. Control in matrix structures is more difficult than in most other forms. Essentially, each member of a project or team will have two managers. One will be the project manager and the other will be the retained control of functional or top management who oversee all projects. This alone can create ambiguity (with each person in the team having two bosses), but coupled with any scarcity in resources which might emerge, such organizations become potentially fraught with conflict as competition between projects is fostered and some teams feel badly treated or unfairly discriminated against whilst others appear to receive preferential treatment.

In our sample of thirty-one charities, only one organization had attempted to adopt a full matrix structure. This is Christian Aid (see Figure 2.3), although others such as Oxfam were actively considering or had seriously considered in the recent past adopting a matrix, or a matrix-like structure. Christian Aid formally adopted its matrix structure in April 1986 although the organization had been working toward

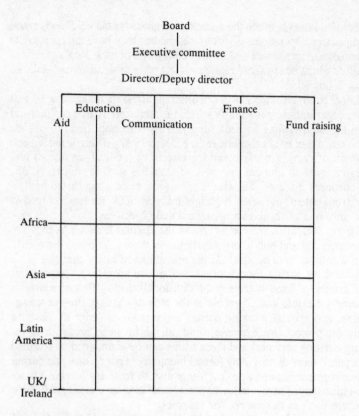

Figure 2.3 Organizational structure: Christian Aid, a matrix structure

this for some time. A case study of Christian Aid is detailed in Chapter 6 later in this book. At this stage, it is sufficient to note that the adoption of the matrix structure has brought both advantages and disadvantages to Christian Aid. In particular, the need for liaison between the various project groups has become more pressing than was at first envisaged and the organization as a whole is more difficult to manage than was envisaged. Christian Aid also presents something of a dilemma to staff and others who are outside the headquarters organization. As one respondent from Area Staff noted:

> When people talk to Christian Aid, they often talk to one person in one section, then another who is probably working on a different project, then another and so on, until they are not sure who is the voice of the organization . . . or indeed if it has one. True central

policy becomes difficult to identify and to unearth.

It is notable that all other organizations in our sample either had functionally differentiated structures or were divisionalized. Despite its theoretical affinity with organized charitable activity, the matrix structure appears to be as rare in this sector as in others.

It should be noted that many charities operate a half-way house toward a matrix structure by operating with two lines of authority. As Brooke (1984) notes, it is quite usual for charities to operate a dual system in which regional offices are accountable both to headquarters and to local membership committees. It is unusual for charities then to move wholly to the stage of structuring their activities around projects and essentially abandoning functional/hierarchical systems. Largely this reluctance appears to stem from two sources. First, managers of charities are aware of some of the problems which might emerge in their own organization, were they to go wholly matrix, although such self-insight, which is often copiously published and distributed in-house, rarely makes comparison with other charities which have addressed similar problems. There seems to be a remarkable lack of organizational learning in this respect.

Second, there are pressures both from internal organization and the external environment of charities which push in a direction away from matrix organization and toward traditional, hierarchical organization. Brooke (1984: 108-11) neatly summarizes these pressures. He argues that they can be traced to the following major factors:

Regulatory bodies and donors

The Charity Commissioners and donors to charities (especially where they are not also members) exercise pressure toward central control and hierarchical structures. Here, both are seeking the ultimate locus of authority and the policy voice of the organization. This is easier to identify in an organization which is structured along more traditional lines. Wilson (1984) also noted the pressure from the Charity Commissioners toward the bureaucratic functioning of charities. This was argued to compound the momentum toward centralization.

Internal organizational forces

This is where the forces for hierarchy and centralization outweigh the forces for a more project oriented organization. Clearly, there are a number of forces which will tend to shift organization structure toward or away from centralization. Brooke (1984) has outlined some of the key stimuli which press for centralization or decentralization. These are summarized below:

Pressures for decentralization:

lack of expertise at head office;
unity of outlook and common purpose across the organization;
need to stimulate local activity;
need to campaign to a greater extent;
lack of urgent controversy.

Pressures to centralize:

constitution over fifty years old (devolution is sometimes not posed as an alternative in older constitutions);
maintaining charitable status;
safeguarding vital knowledge;
irresponsibility or lack of expertise in offices or local branches;
views of donors and registering authorities;
danger of dissension and thus alienating donors and potential donors;
expense of contacting members;
time, effort, and other expenditure on maintaining liaison and co-ordination between offices.

(Adapted from Brooke 1984: 108)

This brief introduction to structure might lead us to believe that any specific structural form adopted by a charity was solely a result of internal and external organizational characteristics. As we have seen, these pressures cannot be ignored, but equally we must remain aware of the possible linkages between *strategy* and *structure*. Following Chandler (1963) and Channon (1973), the link between pursued strategy and resultant structure is a strong bond. In the next section, we explore the concept of strategy and how this might also impact upon the structure of charities.

Strategy in the charitable sector

As we noted in an earlier work, the concept of strategy is not one which is readily associated with organizations in the charitable sector (Wilson and Butler 1986). Commercial organizations pursue strategies in the quest for increased revenue, competitive advantage, and, ultimately, profit. Since these characteristics are not those readily associated with the notion of a charitable organization (Scott 1982), the question of strategy *per se* as relevant to charitable organization is rarely addressed.

Sociologically, the neglect of strategy in charitable and similar organizations, such as communes and some co-operative ventures, rests upon premises and suppositions which are neatly summarized in Tonnies' (1955) distinction between *gesellschaft* and *gemeinschaft*. In *gesellschaft* organizations, authority is founded upon a free contract between individuals or groups of individuals which results in an agreement to recognize and place a master or head above them and to obey either unconditionally or conditionally. In this contract, the individuals in power are assumed to direct and to control the organization. Those held in the labour contract follow and fall in with this managerial strategy since not only are they held in contract but also stand to benefit from the profitable pursuits of the organization. Such benefits can be in the direct form of profit sharing or increased wages (bonuses) or in the retention of a job for a specified period.

Organizations which are characterized as *gesellschaft* naturally presuppose a co-ordinating role for those who are managers since they purchase labour; employ labour; 'sell' labour in the form of value accrued from products. In these organizations, managers are also endowed with the strategic role of steering the organization along the best and most profitable course possible. Indeed, the etymology of the word strategy gives a clue to its association with the management of business enterprises and the *gesellschaft* structure. Derived from the Greek, Latin, and French languages, strategy means 'manoeuvring into favourable positions . . . in particular using a plan in business, etc.' (*Oxford English Dictionary*).

Charitable organizations are not popularly considered to be examples of *gesellschaft*. According to Tonnies (1955: 18–30) such organizations fall into his description of *gemeinschaft*, echoing Plato's *Republic* and *Laws* wherein individuals of a similar mind and ideology come together in collective organizational form to provide a service which either benefits their own collective relationship or, more generally, benefits the populace at large. In particular, Tonnies (1955) identifies *gemeinschaft* with commonwealth and friendship based upon faith, religion, or creed and gives examples of such organizational collectives in the village, the town, and the pivotal role of the church as point of origin. He counterposes this with the more objective and anonymous appropriation of wealth, barter, and exchange and the conducting of business based solely around money. The latter requires a strategy. Collectivity through similarity does not present such a self-evident case.

Historically, too, the elements of managerial strategy are largely absent from the activities of charities. It is more common to find discussions of the emergence of *gemeinschaft* organizations cast in the light of a new political liberalism as societies in Britain and in western Europe and Scandinavia progressed from feudalism to capitalism. It is political ideology which is argued to be the engine of emerging charitable efforts rather than any predetermined managerial plan in the strategic sense. Early associations were reactions against the prevailing *political* modes of thought. Charities espoused liberalism and democratic, participative principles.

Gerlach and Hine (1970) show how this historical context has been sustained into current society, illustrating that charities which might be described as 'new social movements' also do not appear to embrace the concept of strategy. Rather, emphasis is upon co-ordination (by overlapping membership and by friendship ties), communication (horizontal rather than vertical), and control (participants held together in a self-regulating manner based upon common ideological commitment). There are no managerial leaders. Organization is akin to a network in which the activity itself defines and sustains organizational membership rather than any contractual or economic agreement.

Yet such organizations also exist and inter-relate with a larger and wider society and this poses constraints and opportunities for their activities. We have seen already the complex inter-relationship of public agencies, commercial organizations and charities outlined in Chapter 1. In addition, many charities have relatively long organizational lives which means that they have lived through and coped with many aspects of change in their operating domain and in society generally. They have managed, or have been managed, through their history. We turn to the questions which focus upon organizational strategy in the next chapter.

Chapter three

Strategy

Organizations are both chosen by and choose their environments. The choosing of organizations by their environments is witnessed when we observe a firm responding to increased competition, or a water authority opening a new water storage and treatment plant in response to increased demands, or a voluntary organization fund raising in response to an emergency. From this perspective organizations mould themselves around their environments; the new product, the treatment plant or the extra fund-raising unit are all seen as an almost automatic result of events outside the organization. This is the perspective of an open systems model of organization (Katz and Kahn 1966) in which an organization processes inputs to produce outputs and the morphology, or structuration (Giddens 1973), of the organization is a result of what has to be done to achieve this transformation.

More recently, organization theory has refined this image by using a biological metaphor of an organization through ecological or natural selection theory. Here an organization is seen as in competition with other organizations for resources but selects the most appropriate structures to cope with changing conditions (Hannan and Freeman 1977, Weick 1969). Again, organizational adaptation is seen as a somewhat automatic process, of an appropriate structure or sub-structure being selected, as the genes are selected in a biological system, according to the theory of natural selection.

While the above perspective may, over large numbers of organizations, explain a considerable amount of the various actions taken by organizations, it neglects the choices available to decision makers in determining strategy. Decision makers actually have to choose to introduce a new product, choose to open a new water treatment plant, or choose to start a fund-raising campaign. The issue of strategic choice was raised by Child (1972) as a counter to overly deterministic theories and is somewhat similar to the argument found in philosophy, sociology, and psychology concerning the extent to which individual behaviour is an outcome of environment or of choice. In practice both factors operate;

organizations, like individuals, are formed by their environments, but they also choose their environments and act upon them.

Dependence and uncertainty

An organization is a purposive system but in achieving its goals it relies upon its environment for resources. For the firm, this means acquiring capital, raw materials, labour, and so forth. These are transformed in the process of manufacturing or of providing a service. The voluntary organization is no exception. It, too, must create and manage its domain and task environment (Thompson 1967). The task environment consists of those elements in the environment upon which an organization depends and it is managing these dependencies that is a critical task for an organization. In making exchanges in the environment an organization has to satisfy those dominant elements which have power over it and supply vital needs.

In addition to managing dependence an organization has to cope with uncertainty. Uncertainties can arise if a particular resource is unpredictable, if technology is changing quickly, if demands for the organization's services are unpredictable, or if the basic legitimacy of the organization appears to be under threat. For some voluntary organizations the apparently sudden crises in Ethiopia and the Sudan produced uncertainties on two fronts; first, the demands for the services of many Third World charities increased and, second, the increased fund-raising activity started bringing in more funds. The context of Third World charities changed in response to this domain-led stimulus. Of course, the managers of each charity in theory had a strategic choice not to respond, although they would have had to pay regard to the consequences for organizational image in the eyes of both givers and receivers if they had decided on preserving *status quo* as a strategy.

Competitive and co-operative strategies

Given the two basic problems of resolving the critical dependencies and uncertainties that organizations face we start our consideration of how this is done through the notion of strategic choice. We can posit that there are a number of ways in which these dual problems can be resolved. Competition and co-operation represent two broad polar opposites of strategy, each one in itself consisting of a number of sub-types (Thompson 1967). The aim of the following discussion is to elaborate specific elements of strategy based upon the notion of these two generic types.

The competitive strategy is well enshrined in the literature on business policy and a number of different typologies exist. Porter (1980, 1985) has perhaps given the most systematic prescriptive treatment of competitive business strategies. Another well known prescriptive typology is that of the Boston Consulting Group (Shanklin and Ryans 1981), four types corresponding to different combinations of the market share and growth held by an organization. This outline states that a firm needs to maintain a balanced portfolio of businesses. The stars are those products which have high market share and growth and represent the future profits which can be ploughed back for future expansion, the cash cows are those lines that have high market share and low market growth; these lines are mature and about to become the dogs (see below) but for the present provide the cash to finance new ventures. New ventures are those innovative lines which could become tomorrow's stars although there is high risk concerning this possibility; they are seen as possessing high market growth but low market share. The dogs are those lines which have low market share and low market growth and risk becoming a burden upon the company; these are recommended for divestment.

What is not so well represented or prescribed in the business policy literature is the notion of a co-operative strategy and yet this is becoming an increasingly important aspect of modern industrial organization. Joint ventures in aerospace, telecommunications and other industries are used to finance the development of new technology which are both cash and skill hungry (see, for example, Harrigan 1986). In the non-profit sector such co-operation is more vital still. Hospitals have agreements to exchange use of facilities, local authorities form many joint ventures with other organizations both in the non-profit and for-profit sectors, and voluntary organizations are increasingly joining together for fund raising, lobbying, or delivery of services. Voluntary organizations are also increasingly forming joint ventures with the for-profit sector through sponsorship or urban renewal or in many other areas of activity.

In considering types of strategy we can see the task environment of an organization as consisting of three principal types of other organizations. There are those elements which support the organization through provision of resources; in the case of a business these elements may be suppliers of capital, customers or suppliers of raw materials; in the case of a voluntary organization these are the *givers*. The second category of environmental elements are the *commensals*; in business these are more usually known as competitors but the essential feature of a commensal is that it is trying to attract the attention of the pool of supporters for resources. Commensals for a voluntary organization are other voluntary organizations in the same line of activity (industry) and more broadly in the voluntary sector as a whole. Then there are also the *receivers*, which in the case of a voluntary organization do not usually provide revenue but which are nevertheless necessary to legitimate the existence of the organization to the givers.

Competitive strategies

The essence of the competitive strategy is an attempt to manage uncertainty and dependence by alternative maintenance, that is, by ensuring that the organization never has to rely upon a small number of supporters whether this be in terms of customers, clients, or suppliers. For a voluntary organization this means ensuring that there is a a constant pool of givers that can be drawn upon. It might also mean that there is constant source of receivers although this might normally be seen as less critical than the problem of managing the givers. Receivers should not be ignored in the strategic portfolio, however. Organizations such as St Dunstan's which caters for the war blinded is now at a stage where the number of clients is finite and decreasing (see Chapter 6).

Following from the above a number of sub-types of the competitive strategy may be seen:

Efficiency

In business the typical image of a competitive strategy is that of price competition in which a given set of rivals battle it out for a relatively fixed number of customers by reducing prices, by intensive advertising targeted upon specific groups and the like. This is akin to the defender strategy identified by Miles and Snow (1978). If this is not to become a self-destructive process the firm has to set internal goals concentrating upon efficiency of operations and improving internal control. The basic problem is how to do what is already being done more efficiently. Radical innovation is inappropriate since efforts have to go into improving existing products and processes in an incremental way. This is a strategy that is particularly appropriate for a stable and well understood task knowledge and for an environment in which there are many buyers and many sellers (see Quinn 1980). Transferring these ideas to voluntary organizations, we could still envisage the situation where organizations are competing against one another for a relatively fixed pool of funds. One strategic response would be to improve internal operating procedures to improve efficiency and use competitive advertising to maintain and perhaps increase support.

Innovation

A business organization may attempt to move out of direct competition by innovating new products and services. In a sense it is trying to create a monopoly, realizing that this can only be temporary since competitors will follow suit once knowledge about the innovation is diffused. Miles and Snow (1978) define this as the prospector strategy. There are consequences for internal organization in that the emphasis needs now to be upon flexibility rather than efficiency. An organization pursuing innovation is selecting for itself a dynamic environment by seeking customers who require, or can be persuaded to require, change. Change in taste, technology, and needs is the natural environment of an innovative strategy. In the voluntary sector the spur to innovation might come from both the input and output sides. For inputs, organizations may attempt to use new methods of fund raising aimed at an existing pool of givers or may use new techniques to reach new givers. On the output side innovation will attempt to create a new domain of clients or to improve and change the service provided for an existing clientele. Responding to and/or creating change is, of course, one of the key management problems in all organizations.

Co-operative strategies

The literature on business strategy has consistently emphasized the needs for competitive strategy (e.g. Porter 1980, 1985) but neglected to point out that co-operative strategies might be appropriate for particular circumstances. In practice, however, co-operative strategies are frequently found; in the aerospace industry it is common for a firm (such as Rolls-Royce) to form a joint venture with one of their two main rivals for the development of a new engine while competing for customers. Butler and Carney (1983) have used the term 'the managed market' to refer to situations in which firms attempt to control competition through forming various co-operative mechanisms. One example quoted is the construction industry where many sub-contractors are linked with the main contractor through a series of formal agreements which, in their day-to-day operation, require a degree of trust and social interaction which are completely neglected in the theory of competitive strategies.

Thompson (1967) pointed to the co-operative strategy as a means of an organization developing a more stable predictable environment for itself. Some specific processes of co-operation he indicated were:

Co-optation, taking into the management of an organization a member (or members) of the management of another organization as seen in overlapping directorships.

Contracting, a heading under which Thompson included the exchange of formal, legal contracts between organizations and the exchange of less formal social obligations.

Coalescing, in which organizations come together and act as a unit for some unit of activity for a specified time, which may take the form of a joint venture as already discussed or be taken to the point of a merger.

In using co-operation, an organization is trying to gain power over the appropriate element(s) in the environment. For success, this arrangement must reduce uncertainty for both elements through the exchange of obligations. It should be pointed out here that the theory of co-operative strategy espoused assumes relatively equal power between participants. If power were asymmetric, as in a take-over, the terms of the exchange are set by the dominant acquiring organization and this could then hardly be described as an exchange of obligations. A take-over might therefore have to be seen more as an aspect of a competitive strategy whereby an organization is attempting to reduce competition or to extend its customer or supplier base in the case of vertical integration.

The measurement of strategic choice

The measurement of strategy is not simple. Snow and Hambrick (1980) have summarized some of the major methodological problems. One aspect of these problems concerns the definition of strategy and especially the extent to which the concept is seen as a statement of intention or of realization. In this study we are specifically interested in the notion of strategic choice and held this to be best represented by the views of the chief executive officers or the nearest equivalent. Whether or not all those intentions are ultimately achieved would be a matter for further empirical observation.

A further problem concerns the extent to which strategy can be assessed accurately through the eyes of one person. In practice strategy is worked out through a process of pluralist negotiation between a number of powerful people within and outside an organization. Nevertheless, the extent to which chief executives have a clear mental picture of their organization's strategy is still an important dimension of the concept. In the survey part of this study it was the view of the chief executive which we sought. In the case studies, multiple views were taken both from inside and outside the organizations. The analysis thus attempts to provide both depth and breadth as mutually supportive analytical constructs. Documentary and archival data informed both the survey and the case studies.

The elements of strategy

We can now more specifically define and operationalize the elements of strategy. These, according to the above discussion, take into account:

1. The actions of supporters of an organization. That is, those elements which provide resources through the process of environmental exchange. This means that both input and output strategies are required since these are the two sides of an exchange relationship (see Wilson and Butler 1986).

2. The actions of commensals since they compete for a common pool of support.
3. The broad distinction between the characteristics and implications of a competitive strategy and a co-operative strategy as a means of managing dependence and uncertainty.

Method and sample

The thirty-one voluntary organizations selected for this study are involved in three principal industries, Third World aid, visually handicapped, and sea rescue. All organizations were in the top 200 British charities as defined by the Charities Aid Foundation. These three industries were selected for the following reasons.

Third World aid

Third World aid was attracting a lot of media attention at the time of the study due to the Ethiopian and Sudanese famine. This industry represents the gift relationship at its most extreme with donors apparently willing to give money in large amounts to people in far away places who are very remote. In a sense, it is the example of the giving ethic created almost entirely by messages received through television and the press.

Further, it was a situation which was presenting a sizeable strategic problem for some of the organizations involved. All of a sudden they had to manage a sudden influx of funds which presented the danger of what some members of these organizations saw as diverting them from longer term non-disaster relief goals.

Third World aid effectively consists of two sub-groups:

Third World secular international organizations (TWS), that is, UK organizations established to either provide services for, or work with, peoples in less developed overseas countries *including* those who also operate in the UK (e.g. Save the Children Fund, British Red Cross Society) but excluding those known to operate through religious organizations. There are thirteen organizations in this category.

Third World religious aid organizations (TWR), that is, a UK-based organization established to provide either services for, or work with, peoples in less developed overseas countries, that: (a) makes specific mention of the alleviation of poverty or other relief work coupled with specific mention of furthering some religious aim; (b) includes those organizations known to operate solely through religious organizations; (c) also includes those organizations known to operate in the UK also, e.g. Christian Aid. There are five organizations in this category.

Organizations in the visually handicapped industry (VISH)

In contrast, the visually handicapped industry represents that solid foundation of British charitable work stretching far back into the nineteenth century. Here the problems are more easily located in the realm of the everyday problems of living. Most people know of a visually handicapped or even a blind person. This kind of charitable work also has strong links with the state-run health and social services sector.

The sample includes any organization established to provide either services for, or work with, peoples classed as blind or partially sighted, but excluding those organizations involved with general disablement which *may include* blindness. Specific mention of blindness must be made. There are twelve organizations in this category.

Sea rescue (SRES)

The sea rescue charitable industry effectively amounts to one of the largest, oldest, and most prestigious of British charities, the Royal National Lifeboat Institution. This organization was selected because of its policy of independence from government funding.

There is one organization in this category.

Operationalization

This section gives the quantitative analyses of our survey data. The aim is to develop the strategic profiles and the non-statistically inclined reader may wish to move to the Strategic Profile Summaries given on page 47.

A series of eight questions were designed to capture the principal aspects of input and eight questions to capture output strategies and covering both the competitive and co-operative perspectives.

Thus competitive strategies were covered by questions concerning an emphasis upon improving efficacy of existing procedures for delivery of services or for gaining funds, extending tested methods to new givers/receivers, or developing new methods of reaching existing or new givers/receivers.

Co-operative strategies were captured by questions covering the development of joint programmes of a formal or informal nature and developing stable contracting type of relations with givers/receivers, or with other voluntary organizations.

These questions formed part of a wider ranging interview schedule designed to elicit other data from the CEOs and Senior Managers of the sample organizations (see Appendix).

Patterns of strategic choice

The two generic strategies of competition and co-operation and their associated sub-types are ways of managing dependence and uncertainty. Although the business policy literature tends to suggest that an organization needs to be one thing or another, one aspect of this study is to put this assumption to the empirical test. We might anticipate that certain strategic choices are either incompatible with one another or that managements would try to economize by not trying to do too many things at the same time. For instance, at first sight classical economic theory suggests that managers do not choose both to compete and co-operate with the same firms. Yet the expanding theory of co-operative strategies suggests that in some circumstances a company may well compete for the same customers with a rival at the same time as forming a joint venture for the development of a new project. We would anticipate a similar pattern of actions in the voluntary sector.

In order to explore possible patterns in strategies the data were factor analysed, using the principal components method, to explore inter-relationships in the elements of strategy. We found that for input strategies three factors could be distinguished.

Table 3.1 Factor analysis of 8 input strategy variables to give 3 input strategy factors

		Input strategy factor item loadings		
	Strategy variables	*Extension (IEXN)*	*Co-operation (ICOP)*	*Efficiency (IEFF)*
	Extent to which organization emphasizes developing:			
Q				
2	Tested methods to new givers	**0.71**	−0.11	0.49
3	New methods to existing givers	**0.76**	0.05	0.05
4	New methods to new givers	**0.75**	−0.33	−0.14
5	Joint programmes of short duration with commensals	**0.62**	0.20	0.13
6	Joint programmes of short duration with givers	0.00	**0.79**	0.23
7	Long duration programmes with commensals	0.20	**0.56**	−0.51
8	Long duration programmes with givers	−0.49	**0.51**	−0.07
1	Improving efficacy of tested methods	0.19	0.20	**0.85**
	Eigenvalue	2.57	1.43	1.09
	% variance explained	32.1	17.8	13.6

Note: Q number refers to question on original interview schedule (see the Appendix for full question)

The first factor (explaining 32.1 per cent of the variance), which we call the extension strategy, consists of high factor scores on the variables relating to questions of innovation but also including elements of co-operative strategy concerning the development of joint short-term programmes with commensals. This input extension factor is heavily weighted towards the innovation variables but indicates that the voluntary organizations in our sample tended to innovate in conjunction with others in the same industry through short-term rather than long-term programmes. In fact, there is a negative factor loading for long duration programmes with givers, emphasizing further the short duration of these innovation programmes. This factor supports the proposition outlined above that voluntary organizations can both compete *and* co-operate but that the co-operation tends to be around specific issues and projects which are relatively short lived.

The second factor accounts for 17.8 per cent of the variance and is heavily weighted towards three of the co-operative variables. This input co-operation strategy shows that organizations which enter into short duration joint programmes with givers also tend to have longer term programmes with commensals and with givers. We call this the co-operative strategy which indicates an emphasis on the nexus of co-operative procedures with givers and commensals.

The final factor accounting for 13.6 per cent of the variance primarily comprises those elements relating to improving the efficacy of existing methods of gaining inputs. We call this the input efficiency strategy. It should also be noted that this factor is fairly heavily weighted on the variable relating to the use of tested methods to new givers, indicating that it could form the springboard of an overall competitive strategy. The -0.51 factor loading with long-term duration programmes with commensals shows that the pursuit of efficiency tends not to be compatible with the pursuit of co-operation in our sample of voluntary organizations.

As far as input strategies are concerned, this factor analysis gives some support for the notion of two distinct groups of strategy, namely the competitive and co-operative types. When we come to the output strategies this picture is maintained but with some important differences.

Output strategies

The strongest factor (explaining 30.0 per cent of the variance) consists of the four competitive variables. We simply call this the output extension strategy (see Table 3.2). The co-operation variables tend to fall into two groups. First is commensal co-operation (22.0 per cent of the variance) which is most strongly weighted on the variables measuring joint programmes (both long and short term). Second is a factor (15.2 per cent of the variance) which is capturing the notion of client co-operation due to its strong weighting on the variables measuring joint programmes with clients, both short and long term.

Table 3.2 Factor analysis of 8 output strategy variables to give 3 output strategy factors

		Output strategy factor item loadings		
	Strategy variables	Extension (OEXN)	Commensal co-operation (OCMC)	Client co-operation (OCLC)
	Extent to which organization emphasizes developing:			
Q				
1	Efficacy of delivering existing services	**0.69**	0.10	−0.03
2	Tested services to new clients	**0.66**	−0.14	0.47
3	New services, existing clients	**0.49**	0.69	−0.01
4	New services, new clients	**0.75**	0.13	0.04
5	Joint programmes short duration with commensals	0.34	**0.78**	0.03
7	Joint programmes long duration with commensals	−0.26	**0.82**	−0.01
6	Joint programmes short duration with clients	0.29	−0.25	**0.72**
8	Joint programmes long duration with clients	−0.20	0.31	**0.82**
	Eigenvalue	2.40	1.76	1.22
	% variance explained	30.0	22.0	15.2

Note: Q number refers to question on original interview schedule (see the Appendix for full question)

We should point to an apparent anomaly in defining the second factor as commensal co-operation, since there is also a heavy weighting on new services to existing receivers. This suggests that an important aspect of commensal co-operation for our sample of voluntary organizations is in aiming this strategy at new services for receivers.

Relationships between input and output strategies

An appropriate question is to ask whether there is any connection between input and output strategies. This will be dealt with in greater detail below when discussing the cluster analysis but a preliminary analysis can be made here. Table 3.3 presents the Pearson correlations between the three input and three output strategy factor variables. None of these is significant. The indications so far suggest that input and output strategies are mutually quite independent.

Table 3.3 Pearson's correlation between input and output strategy factors

		Input strategies		
		IEXN	ICOP	IEFF
	OEXN	0.188	0.203	-0.082
Output strategies	OCMC	-0.102	0.298	0.065
	OCLC	0.098	0.180	-0.044

All significance levels at $p > 0.31$ $n = 31$.

IEXN — Input extension	OEXN — Output extension
ICOP — Input co-operation	OCMC — Output commensal co-operation
IEFF — Input efficiency	OCLC — Output client co-operation

Clusters of strategies

While factor analysis allows us to find patterns between variables it does not allow us to identify a pattern of strategy for individual organizations. The evidence suggests that we would be justified in replacing the sixteen original constituent variables of strategy by three input strategic factors (extension, co-operation, and efficiency) and by three output strategic factors (competition, commensal co-operation, and client co-operation). These six factors now become the characteristics of strategy and we can now proceed to describe the strategies pursued by our sample organizations through the use of cluster analysis.

Clustering is a way of finding patterns between organizations according to their scores on a number of variables. For the sample of thirty-one organizations, it is possible to conceive of anything from thirty-one distinct clusters, when every organization has a different strategic profile, to one cluster, when all the organizations are the same. Neither of these two extremes is very useful or interesting because it either tells us that all organizations are unique (which is what chief executives often like to think!) or that all organizations are the same (which is often what naive outsiders think).

As a statistical technique, cluster analysis starts from the assumption that all the thirty-one organizations are different and then examines which two organizations can most sensibly be placed together using the information provided by the six strategy factors. A number of different procedures and configurations were tried and we eventually identified five clusters consisting of nine, five, ten, four, and three organizations respectively as having both conceptual and statistical meaning. Our definition of these five clusters was not taken purely upon statistical grounds as we also included a considerable amount of non-statistical information which we had collected during our investigation.

In order to test the validity of our clusters two kinds of statistical analysis were used. First, the six strategic variables were used in a discriminant analysis to predict cluster membership of the full sample of thirty-one organizations. This gave a 93 per cent correct prediction. A three-quarter sub-sample was then selected and cluster membership re-predicted on this sub-sample and the remaining one-quarter sub-sample. The predictions were 92 per cent and 78 per cent correct respectively which was considered a sufficient confirmation of our chosen clustering using this statistical method.

Table 3.4 Discriminant analysis

Strategy factor	Function			
	1	2	3	
Inputs				
Extension (IEXN)	0.82	0.62	−0.05	
Co-operation (ICOP)	0.09	−0.23	0.10	
Efficiency (IEFF)	−0.75	0.68	0.34	
Outputs				
Efficiency and extension (OEXN)	0.83	−0.35	0.41	
Commensal co-operation (OCMC)	0.12	−0.37	0.57	
Client co-operation (OCLC)	0.09	0.07	0.75	
Cluster group				*n*
1 Extenders (EX)	2.72	0.19	−0.10	9
2 Competitive co-operators (CC)	1.03	−0.38	1.75	5
3 Output co-operators (OC)	−0.90	0.53	0.81	10
4 Acquisitors (AQ)	−3.52	1.71	−1.28	4
5 Reactors (RE)	−2.20	−3.96	−0.81	3
				Total: 31

Predicted group membership, 94 per cent correct

The second statistical test used was to compute the strategic variable means for each cluster and to conduct a one-way analysis of variance on these means across the clusters. Table 3.5 shows the means. The analysis of variance showed significant differences at the $p < 0.005$ level for all strategy factors except for input co-operation which is significant at the $p < 0.10$ level.

Table 3.5 Strategic profiles of clusters: strategic factor means (standardized) by cluster

Strategic factor		Cluster					
		1 EX	2 CC	3 OC	4 AQ	5 RE	
Inputs							
EXTN —	Extending to givers + temporary commensal co-operation	**0.86**	**0.38**	**−0.19**	**−0.31**	**−2.16**	< 0.001
COOP —	Temporary and durable giver co-operation	−0.21	**1.02**	−0.21	−0.48	0.25	< 0.10
EFFN —	Efficiency	**−0.82**	0.39	0.33	**1.41**	−1.16	< 0.001
Outputs							
EFEX —	Efficiency and extending to receivers	0.42	**0.99**	−0.34	**−1.13**	−0.25	< 0.005
CPCM —	Commensal co-operation	**−0.60**	**1.24**	−0.21	−0.11	0.57	< 0.01
CPCL —	Receiver co-operation	−0.26	0.10	**0.90**	**−1.32**	−0.62	< 0.001
	Mean	−0.10	0.69	0.05	−0.32	−0.56	
	n =	9	5	10	4	3	= 31

Cluster labels: EX = Extenders; CC = Competitive co-operators; OC = Output co-operators; AQ = Acquisitors; RE = Reactors

Cluster descriptions

Descriptions of each cluster group may now be drawn up. A cluster represents a pattern of averages for the six strategy factors but each cluster consists of individual organizations which will vary around the central mean pattern. Membership of a cluster is justified by the notion that an organization will have more in common, as far as strategy is concerned, with the average of its clusters than with the average of the other clusters.

Table 3.5 now allows us to put some meaning to the strategies pursued within each cluster group. From this table we can see the strategy variables which stand out for each cluster as being particularly high or low as these are highlighted in bold numbers. In this way we can develop strategic profiles for the organizations. Another aspect which is relevant from Table 3.5 is the mean score of all six variables for each cluster. These range from the high of 0.69 for cluster 2 and the low of −0.56 for cluster 5. A high score suggests an overall high strategic profile for the cluster; the organizations in cluster 2, for instance, are actively pursuing a greater range of strategies, as measured by the strategy variables, than are the organizations in cluster 5.

The strategic profile summaries

The strategic profiles can now be summarized under five distinct groupings, or clusters, as shown by the statistical analysis. These clusters form the basis for subsequent discussion of strategy.

Cluster 1: The extenders (EX)

Summary: Extend to new givers with temporary commensal input co-operation but with low output temporary commensal co-operation. Low concern with input efficiency. Slightly below average strategic profile. This is a specialised strategic profile. Organization membership, 9 (5 Third World secular, 0 Third World religious, 4 visually handicapped, 0 sea rescue).

Cluster 2: The competitive co-operators (CC)

Summary: Very high giver and commensal co-operation for inputs combined with output competition. Highest strategic profile. Organization membership, 5 (2 Third World secular, 1 Third World religious, 2 visually handicapped, 0 sea rescue).

Cluster 3: The output co-operators (OC)

Summary: Highest client co-operation and fairly high on input efficiency. Generally low to average on other factors. Average strategic profile. Organization membership, 10 (5 Third World secular, 3 Third World religious, 2 visually handicapped, 0 sea rescue).

Cluster 4: The acquisitors (AQ)

Summary: Very high concern with improving existing methods of gaining inputs. Very low concern with competition for new receivers or with receiver co-operation. Low strategic profile. Organization membership, 4 (1 Third World secular, 0 Third World religious, 2 visually handicapped, 1 sea rescue).

Cluster 5: The reactors (RE)

Summary: Very low concern with gaining inputs either by extending to new givers or by improving existing methods. Low extension to receivers and client co-operation. Organization membership, 3 (0 Third World secular, 1 Third World religious, 2 visually handicapped, 0 sea rescue).

Industry effects

Table 3.6 shows the distribution of organization by industry in each cluster. If each industry was represented according to the proportion of member organizations in the overall sample there would be no industry by cluster effect. Assuming this to be the null hypothesis, analysis of the actual versus estimated frequency in each industry/cluster cell shows an industry effect which can be seen due to the influence of Third World secular and Third World religious industries. Cluster 1 has a higher proportion of the secular organizations than of the religious organizations. This is the extending strategy and indicates that the religious organizations are less likely to reach out to new givers in particular, although they may be more concerned with efficiency. The secular Third World Aid organizations exhibit considerably greater tendency towards this extending strategy.

Table 3.6 Strategy cluster by industry

Cluster	TWS		*Industry* TWR		VISH		SRES		
EX	(3.77)	5	(1.45)	0	(3.48)	4	(0.29)	0	9
CC	(2.10)	2	(0.81)	1	(1.94)	2	(0.16)	0	5
OC	(4.19)	5	(1.61)	3	(3.87)	2	(0.32)	0	10
AQ	(1.88)	1	(0.65)	0	(1.55)	2	(0.13)	1	4
RE	(1.25)	0	(0.48)	1	(1.16)	2	(0.10)	0	3
		13		5		12		1	31

Notes: Numbers thus ( ) refer to estimated number of organizations in each cluster/industry cell. Other numbers refer to actual number of organizations.

TWS = Third World secular; TWR = Third World religious; VISH = visually handicapped; SRES = sea rescue

In strategy cluster 3, we see nearly the opposite situation with TWR organizations showing an above average representation. This is the output co-operating strategy which indicates a greater willingness by religious organizations to co-operate with clients than the average. Both Third World religious and Third World secular organizations show a below average competitive co-operation in all other ways (cluster 2) and below average non-competitive strategies (cluster 4) but an average representation in the very small cluster 5, non-extending strategy.

The visually handicapped industry is notable for its even representation across strategy clusters confirming our initial description of the industry as a mature and solid sectoral representative of the British voluntary sector.

Managing the institutional environment

So far the discussion has mainly considered how a voluntary organization manages its task environment. Equally important, however, is the effect the institutional environment can have upon it. By the institutional environment we mean that aspect of the environment which is setting the basic values, norms, and rules within which an organization operates. For voluntary organizations the legal framework of charities is a key factor. This involves the total assemblage of rules and regulations which have grown up over centuries and which since the mid nineteenth century the Charity Commissioners enforce as we have described above.

Today, the institutional environment, especially for the larger well-known charities, goes much further than this. Charities often receive a large amount of their income from governmental sources. Charities are seen pressing government for more resources on many occasions or to take remedial action in other ways to support a cause whether this be for more aid to the Third World, increases in allowances for handicapped people, changes in tax law, and the like.

There is an increasing organizational literature (e.g. Meyer and Rowan 1977) which sees managing the institutional environment as a key aspect of an organization's strategy. We attempted to capture this by encouraging CEOs to describe their approach to the direct lobbying of government. Their replies were coded, first as to the frequency of lobbying activities (lobbying activity), and second as to the degree of co-operation with other voluntary organizations in carrying out this lobbying (lobbying co-operation).

Pearson's correlations of these two lobbying variables and the six strategy factors reveal no significant correlations even at $p < 0.10$ (Table 3.7). When the means of the lobbying variables are calculated for each

Table 3.7 Pearson's correlation, governmental lobbying and strategy factors

	Lobbying activity LOBB	Lobbying co-operation LOCO
Input strategy		
IEXN	0.14	0.18
ICOP	0.18	0.15
IEFF	−0.13	0.22
Output strategy		
OEXN	−0.24	−0.12
OCMC	0.03	0.05
OCLC	0.23	0.09

$n = 31$. All correlations $p > 0.10$.

strategy cluster (Table 3.8) we see again no apparent relationship with strategy type treating each cluster separately. However, if we contrast lobbying activity of clusters 1, 2, and 3 with 5 and 5 we see that 4 and 5 combined have a tendency towards lower lobbying activity than clusters 1, 2, and 3 combined. We also see that cluster 5 has lower lobbying co-operation. These results indicate that the reactors and acquisitors have a greater tendency to indulge in lobbying.

Table 3.8 Lobbying and strategy clusters: ANOVA cluster means (standardized variables)

	Strategy cluster					
	1 EX	2 CC	3 OC	4 AQ	5 RE	
Lobbying activity	−0.05	−0.16	0.31	−0.22	−0.31	$p > 0.83$ 1, 2, 3: cf. 4.5 $p < 0.10$
Lobbying co-operation	−0.13	0.07	0.07	0.36	−0.46	$p > 0.86$ 1, 2, 3, 4: cf. 5 < 0.10

Cluster labels: EX = Extenders; CC = Competitive co-operators; OC = Output co-operators; AQ = Acquisitors; RE = Reactors

Summary

This chapter has concentrated upon finding a framework for describing and measuring the strategy of an organization that can be meaningful for drawing comparisons between organizations. The derived cluster groupings represent patterns of strategy seen in this particular sample of voluntary organizations. There is no reason to suppose that a different sample would show a similar pattern. The data emphasize the great diversity of strategic choices available to the managers of voluntary organizations.

Chapter four

Context, strategy, and structure

Introduction

There is an inherent danger in ascribing simple causal links between strategic choice and strategic clusters revealed in the data. Of course, such linkages are empirically possible, but their meaning is questionable. To do so would merely shed light upon one dimension of the voluntarist–determinist debates, pivoting around the notion of strategic choice. The real world of strategy formation in charities is far more complex than an analysis of strategic choice can reveal, however deep such analysis goes.

We have already mentioned the special managerial difficulties presented by the gift relationship and, indeed, by the political economy of the voluntary sector overall (see Wilson and Butler 1985). In addition, many charities are characterized by their organizational cultures (Pettigrew 1979) which are dominantly moral, self-reflexive, democratic, participative, and altruistic. It is these inner cultures which pervade and motivate the management of strategy in charities. Ideological, cultural, and sometimes religious beliefs act as powerful constraints and guides for organizational strategies. So the managers of charities not only have to steer their strategic way around the contingent dependencies depicted in the previous chapter, but they also have to manage the wider political environment and the inner culture of their own organization. We refer to culture and environment together as *context* in this chapter.

Authors who inhabit the prescriptive school of organizational strategy (e.g. Porter 1980, 1985) have largely ignored the impact of context, assuming the strategic decision-making process to be rational, planned, purposive, and processually linear. However, substantial empirical and theoretical studies have indicated the fallacy of such assumptions. Hickson *et al.* (1986) demonstrated that many strategic decisions were processed through organizations in arenas which were politically charged with competing interests which prevailed over any 'rational' objectivity.

Linearity was equally dispelled as a glorified ideal in an earlier work by Mintzberg *et al.* (1976) and Hickson *et al.* (1986) similarly illustrated the circuitous nature of process. In very recent studies, authors such as Pettigrew (1987) and Whipp *et al.* (1987) have emphasized the importance of 'inner and outer context' as they form integral parts of the strategic tapestry. Outer context refers to national, economic, political, and social prevalences whilst inner context reflects organizational cultures and structures. In an extension of this approach, Rojek and Wilson (1987) have argued that international context is equally a factor which impinges upon the management of strategy. Taking a 'world system' perspective, they argue that dominantly capitalist market characteristics (amongst other factors) mitigate against the survival of co-operative forms of organization in Yugoslavia.

Whether or not the reader takes a national or an international perspective, the need to take context into account seems unquestionable. We turn to contextual elements next.

Organizational contexts

When seeking contextual explanations of strategy the business policy literature is strangely silent. There are statements like 'stick to the knitting' (Peters and Waterman 1982), meaning that the successful business should concentrate upon doing a few related things well but this is presented as a universal statement. There are exceptions. Miles and Snow (1978), for instance, attach specific environmental and operational conditions to their three types of strategy. The 'defender' strategy is seen as appropriate for stable, relatively concentrated environments and operations while the 'prospector' is a more appropriate strategy for changing environmental and operating conditions.

Thompson (1967) took a broader contingent view of strategy. His argument can be summarized by outlining three main co-operative strategies which are suitable for particular combinations of dependence upon commensals and supporters:

Contracting

Contracting refers to the negotiation of agreements for future performances. A contract can be a formal agreement between a supplier and a buying organization to provide so much of a good at a specified price, of a specified quality, and at a specified time. It can also include less formal arrangements, such as an understanding between a benefactor and a charity that, for instance, a lifeboat, a building, or a 'parcel' of aid is associated with the benefactor's name.

According to Thompson contracting is a suitable strategy for high commensal and support concentration. Under this condition an organization becomes dependent upon a small number of supporters and yet is in competition with a small number of commensals. As Thompson argues, we are likely to see contracting as a means of managing dependence and uncertainty when the organization's principal problem is that of ensuring that the small number of supporters do not lose interest.

Co-opting

Co-opting is the process whereby an organization absorbs new elements into its management as a means of 'averting threats to its stability or existence' (Thompson, 1967:35). Firms co-opt members of financial institutions in the expectation of gaining more favourable terms. Charities co-opt prominent people in the expectation of increasing their prestige and therefore the flow of inputs.

But co-opting can be constraining to an organization because the co-opted can impose conditions. Hence co-opting is a strategy more likely to be adopted by organizations which are weak in relation to critical elements in the environment.

Thompson suggests that co-optation is suitable for dispersed commensals and concentrated support: here the organization is fundamentally weak since it has reliance upon a single supporter but there are many other organizations vying for this same support. In this situation an organization may attempt to manage dependence and uncertainty by co-opting into its management people who are likely to be sympathetic to the aims of the organization's management and who can provide a special expertise.

Coalescing

Coalescing refers to a joint venture or some other form of coalition with another organization. Joint ventures, common in high-technology industries such as aerospace, and increasingly amongst some large voluntary organizations, involve an agreement (usually formal) for the sharing of facilities, products, resources, or information for a specified time or project. Coalescing can be less formalized such as when a number of voluntary organizations agree on a joint approach to fund raising.

Coalescing is suitable when commensal and supporters are concentrated but more power is needed than in contracting.

Some attempts have been made to test these propositions for industrial organizations. Pfeffer and Salancik (1978) examined the conditions under which firms form joint ventures with others in the same industry finding that such projects tend to occur in environments of intermediate concentration. Butler and Carney (1983) describe the process of managing dependence and uncertainty through four case studies. One case was the construction of a North Sea oil project which required the managing of a very complex environment through a whole network of formal and tacit agreements. In the voluntary sector we would anticipate a similar process at work although we know of no systematic attempt to research the subject.

The variables of context[1]

The specific variables of context used in this study are now presented. In this operationalization some contextual elements are perceptual from respondents whilst others derive from the use of published and archival sources concerning sectoral and organizational data.

Significant others

One measure of the linkages an organization has in its environment is the number of organizations competing for resources in a given industry. For inputs, all charities, broadly, can be seen as competing for the same pool of resources, but on the output side, charities form distinct niches or industries and we have selected four such industries. The industries are Third World overseas aid secular (TWS), visually handicapped (VISH), Third World overseas aid religious (TWR), and sea rescue (SRES), comprising respectively 12, 11, 7, and 1 organizations. SRES represents the most highly concentrated industry and the two Third World sub-industries the least concentrated. VISH gives an intermediate level of concentration.

In many disciplines, the concept of industry is by no means well defined, since firms can cross 'industry' boundaries in their trading. In the voluntary sector, the concept of industry is even less well defined. What our statistical sources define as an industry boundary may not be seen as such by management of member organizations so we also developed a perceptual measure of *concentration*. To test this, chief executives were asked an open-ended question as to which other voluntary organizations were seen as the 'significant others' in their domain. This question was further explained as trying to gain an understanding of which other voluntary organizations they took account of in determining their strategies. Answers to this question indicated: the number of other organizations mentioned, that is, mentions given (G); and the number of times each organization received a mention, that is, mentions received (R). From Tables 4.1 and 4.2 we can see the results of this analysis. One notable feature is that there is considerable cross referencing of Third World secular and Third World religious organizations, suggesting that they do not act wholly as separate industries. Further, we note that the average number of mentions received is more than three per organization in the case of the Third World organizations but only one and a half in the case of visually handicapped. This suggests a more

Table 4.1 Chief executives' perception of 'significant others' in the Third World industry

Industry code	Organization code																			Mentions received (R)
	TWS	TWS	TWS	TWS	TWS	TWS	TWS	TWS	TWS	TWR	TWS	TWS	TWS	VSR	TWR	TWR	TWR	TWR	VSH	
	1	2	3	4	5	6	7	8	9	10	11	12	13	14	15	16	17	18	19	
1		x		x	x	x	x			x	x			x						8
2	x			x	x	x	x	x		x	x			x				x		10
3																				0
4					x					x	x			x				x		5
5	x				x					x					x			x		5
6					x															1
7	x				x									x						3
8																				0
9					x															1
10					x										x					2
11																				0
12					x													x		2
13																				0
14	x			x	x	x	x								x					6
15					x	x										x		x		4
16					x	x	x	x							x					5
17					x															1
18																				0
19	x																			1
a					x															1
b																				0
c					x															1
d					x	x										x				3
e																x		x		2
f			x														x			2
g																				0
h																	x			1
(G)	5	1	1	6	15	5	4	1	0	4	3	0	0	4	4	3	2	6	0	

(G) = mentions given

Total given = 64
mean/org = 2.91

Total received = 63
mean/org = 2.24

Notes: 19 is a visually handicapped organization operating in Third World.
a–h are miscellaneous mentioned but not in sample.

Table 4.2 Chief executives' perception of 'significant others' in the field — visually handicapped

Industry code	V S H 20	V S H 21	V S H 22*	V S R 23	V S H 24	V S H 25	V S H 26*	V S H 27	V S H 28	V S H 29+	V S H 30	V S H 31	Mentions received (R)
20		x	x	x		x	x		x		x	x	8
21	x		x										2
22	x	x		x	x								4
23	x	x											2
24			x										1
25													0
26													0
27													0
28							x						1
29													0
30													0
31													0
a‡												x	1
Mentions given	3	3	3	2	1	1	2	0	1	0	1	2	19 = total given

Total given = 19
mean/org = 1.58

Total received = 19
mean/org = 1.58

Notes: *View of marketing director.
+ Mentioned by organization.
‡ Miscellaneous organization mentioned but not interviewed.

outward, industry perspective for the Third World organizations. Analysis of variance also shows no significant difference for mentions given or received across all five clusters separately (Table 4.3). However, when cluster AQ (the acquisitors) is contrasted to the mean of the other four clusters combined we see a significant difference, thereby supporting the above argument that organizations in cluster AQ are in a niche.

At this point reference should be made to the use of analysis of variance in Table 4.3. This technique allows us to compare the means of the five clusters upon any variable and to test whether there is a statistically significant difference in these means. Often, however, there may not be a difference when treating each of the clusters separately but a significant difference can be observed if clusters are grouped together. This can be done using a 'contrasts' measure. Hence, if we

Table 4.3 ANOVA strategy cluster by contextual variables

	Strategy cluster					
	1 EX	2 CC	3 OC	4 AQ	5 RE	
Contextual variable	Dynamic	Service	Dynamic	Niche	Protected	Significance and contrasts
Significant others						
Mentions given	2.5	2.8	3.9	0.5	2.3	$p > 0.31$ 1, 2, 3, 5 cf 4; $p < 0.001$
Mentions received	2.0	2.0	3.6	0	2.0	$p > 0.26$ 1, 2, 3, 5 cf 4; $p < 0.001$
Dependence, receiver	0.05	0.12	−0.19	0.60	−0.52	$p > 0.64$
Dependence, giver	0.50	−0.47	0.12	−0.32	−1.06	$p > 0.18$ 1, 3 cf 2, 4, 5; $p < 0.009$
Voluntary sector share	0.38	−0.29	0.04	−0.16	−0.46	$p > 0.70$ 1, 3 cf 2, 4, 5; $p < 0.16$
Voluntary sector share change	0.25	−0.27	0.16	−0.05	−0.61	$p > 0.72$ 1, 3 cf 2, 4, 5; $p < 0.10$(?)
Income change	0.26	−0.26	0.17	−0.22	−0.55	$p > 0.71$ 1, 3 cf 2, 4, 5; $p < 0.12$ 3 cf 5; $p < 0.07$
Covenant income ($n = 24$)	−0.23	0.20	0.43	−0.25	−0.33	$p > 0.70$ 2, 3 cf 1, 4, 5; $p < 0.12$
Legacy income ($n = 22$)	−0.13	−0.36	−0.30	0.83	0.82	$p > 0.35$ 1, 2, 3 cf 4, 5; $p > 0.32$
Reserves	0.20	−0.50	−0.24	−0.26	1.42	$p < 0.07$
Operations uncertainty	0.32	−0.10	0.07	−0.64	−0.20	$p > 0.62$
Operations variability	−0.21	0.10	0.03	−0.12	0.53	$p > 0.86$
Norm service	−0.11	1.04	−0.49	0.19	0.34	$p < 0.10$
Norm efficiency	0.37	−0.22	−0.53	0.58	0.19	1, 4, 5 cf 2, 3 $p < 0.06$

Notes: $n = 31$ unless otherwise stated.

All variables are standardized.

EX = Extenders; CC = Competitive co-operators; OC = Output co-operators; AQ = Acquisitors; RE = Reactors

take mentions given as an example, the five clusters do not show a significant difference in means when treated separately ($p > 0.31$) but if clusters 1, 2, 3, 5 are added together and contrasted to cluster 4 only, we do see a significant difference ($p < 0.001$). This enables us to say that cluster 4 has a lower mentions given than all the other clusters put together.

Givers and receivers

Another aspect of dependency is the extent to which an organization relies upon a small number of resource providers. As already discussed, because of the separation between the givers and receivers in a voluntary organization, we need to consider both these aspects with the expectation that strategy might be more influenced by the input rather than the output side.

For inputs, assessment was made of the percentage of funds coming from the two largest givers, and in the case of outputs the percentage of funds accounted for by the largest receivers. From these data we were able to compute an input and output dependence profile by creating scale points made up of a range of percentages (see the Appendix). High percentages in relation to a giver or receiver denote high dependence.

Analysis of variance shows no significant effect of strategy clusters on receiver dependence ($p > 0.63$). Giver dependence shows no significant variation across all five clusters ($p > 0.18$) but when we group strategy cluster CC, AQ, and RE and compare this to clusters EX and OC we find a significant difference ($p < 0.009$, Table 4.3). Clusters CC, AQ and RE show a low giver dependence compared to clusters EX and OC. Considering the strategies pursued by Extenders (cluster EX) we see that here the method of coping with giver dependence is through extending and innovating on the input side. For output co-operators (cluster OC) input dependence is actively managed through improving efficiency.

Combining this finding with the data on significant others we build a picture of organizations in cluster AQ existing in a context of low significant others and low giver dependence. A relatively benign environment is suggested with little perceived competition and lower than average giver dependence.

How is this contextual pattern reflected in the strategies? Clusters AQ and RE have a number of features in common which fit this picture. First is a low strategic profile (-0.24 and -0.56 in Table 3.5 respectively) showing that these chief executives see the strategies of their organization as exhibiting a lesser concern with strategy as a whole. We also see from Table 3.5 a low concern with input extension and output competition. This pattern fits a contextual explanation of strategy in that a benign environment would lead to a lesser general concern with innovation and efficiency, the distinguishing features of these strategies.

Voluntary sector share and income

When we look at other financial measures we see a somewhat similar pattern. Voluntary sector share was assessed for each organization using total income (voluntary plus non-voluntary income) as a percentage of the overall voluntary sector income. Standardized measures were used so the figures in Table 4.3 do not represent actual percentages. We can see that there is no significant difference across clusters (Table 4.3).

Voluntary sector share, however, does show a difference when we contrast clusters EX and OC with CC, AQ and RE since the latter clusters show a lower than average share. A similar picture is seen when we use measures of the change in voluntary sector share and of total income change. Clusters EX and OC appear as having higher than average financial growth than clusters CC, AQ, and RE. This is not altogether surprising. The acquisitors (cluster AQ) are in an environmental niche, whereas the reactors (cluster RE) have a cushioned or protected environment.

Another aspect of income is the extent to which it comes from covenants and legacies. Both are used extensively in the voluntary sector. Covenants can be seen as a form of contracting and although this still accounts for a small proportion of income, it is receiving increasing emphasis partly because of recent changes in legislation making it possible for British employees to follow the American pattern of covenanting through payroll deduction schemes. Covenant income does not show a significant difference across all five clusters taken separately.

Clusters EX, AQ, and RE when compared with CC and OC show a tendency to lower covenant income, although we have to accept that the confidence in this result is reduced to some missing data. The sample size here is twenty-four instead of thirty-one with two, three and one missing cases in clusters CC, OC and AQ respectively.

Legacy income is another way of establishing inputs. Whereas covenants provide a known, relatively stable income on the assumption that they are contracts made for four years, legacies can come 'out of the blue' although some organizations seem more able to attract this form of income than others. Legacy income does not show any significant variance across the five clusters treated separately but using the contrasts between clusters EX, CC, and OC combined compared to AQ and RE shows a lower level of legacy income. Again, the confidence in this finding is reduced by missing data with a sample of only 22 instead of 31; 2, 2, 3, 1 and 1 cases missing in the clusters as taken in the above order. Nevertheless, the data indicate that the clusters 4 (AQ) and 5 (RE) have somewhat more benign environments since legacy income is a means of controlling uncertainty and dependence.

Income change

Table 4.3 also gives the income change for the five strategy clusters. Clusters AQ and RE have below average income change. This further supports the analysis of these groups as existing in a relatively static unchanging environment.

Reserves

One way in which an organization can reduce its environmental dependence is by having a high degree of reserves. An organization which could live entirely off reserves would no longer be an open system and could perform according to closed system prescriptions showing concern only for internal operations and maintaining a steady state.

An estimate of the concept of reserves was achieved by taking the Charities' Aid Foundation (CAF) data for capital reserves as a percentage of total income and the results are presented in Table 4.3 as standardized amounts. There is a significant difference across all five groups ($p < 0.064$) with cluster 5 (RE) exhibiting a very high reserve figure. This helps us to explain the low concern with input efficiency already noted with regard to cluster RE, whereas cluster 4 (AQ) is below average in this respect and scores highest of all clusters on input efficiency. Here we observe a distinction between cluster 5 and cluster 4 which exhibits quite a low reserve figure.

Operations

Internal contextual factors include the operations used for converting inputs into outputs. To measure this, chief executives were asked to rate their own organization on a typology based upon Perrow's (1970) schema of technology. Instead of trying to determine directly a modal technology each organization was rated as the extent to which it exhibited routine, engineering (or modular), craft or non-routine technologies, a definition of each being presented as follows:

Routine. Stable task with well defined and analysable methods.
Modular. Variable task with methods well defined.
Craft. Task presented stable with unclear and unanalysable means of achieving it.
Non-routine. Task presented variable and means unclear.

The results were factor analysed to test for major dimensions (see Table 4.4). Two factors can be clearly defined. The first captures the notion of *operating uncertainty* (OPUN) with high negative loadings on well-defined means, a high positive loading on undefined means, and low loadings on *task variability*. The second factor reflects the notion of task variability (OPVR).

From Table 4.3 we can see that operating uncertainty is lowest in cluster AQ, with cluster RE second lowest, and highest in cluster 1 but

Table 4.4 Factor analysis operations

Operating variable	Operating factor	
	OPUN *Uncertainty*	OPVR *Variability*
Routine: stable task, defined means	−0.96	−0.26
Craft: stable task, undefined means	0.77	−0.55
Modular: variable task, defined means	0.14	0.96
Non-routine: variable task, undefined means	0.17	0.01
% variance	39.0	32.3
Eigen value	1.56	1.29

these differences are not statistically significant. Similarly, the pattern for operating variability shows no significant difference across clusters.

Norms

The beliefs and values that participants in an organization hold will affect the decisions that are made concerning the overall goals and strategic choices. We use the term 'norm' to refer to the set of beliefs that guides participants' behaviour. We have not attempted to measure norms as an all-pervasive organizational climate (as the concept of organizational culture is sometimes used) but as those beliefs which are perceived by the chief executive. We wished to see how the chief executives viewed the dominant norms of their organizations since this is what is most likely to constrain or enhance their stated view of organizational strategy.

We start from Thompson's (1967: 84) notion that 'cultures provide general standards of desirability' against which the effect of actions can be evaluated. Organizations create these standards over time and as a result of their internal activities and their attempts to adapt to, and manipulate, various environmental domains.

Any system of assessment requires a yardstick. As a starting point, we can think of this yardstick as having two dimensions, each relating to two problems encountered in measuring anything. First is the comparative/absolute dimension; in deciding whether organization X is performing well, do assessors hold an absolute belief of what is good or bad regardless of what other people are doing? Second is the crystallized/ambiguous dimension: in deciding whether organization X is performing well do assessors have available to them precise empirical measures as to what is good or bad?

A combination of these two dimensions of the assessment process gives us four possible types of norms.

Economic norms are those where beliefs are comparative and crystallized. In assessing the economic performance of a company as good or bad we can only compare it with other companies in the same industry. *Bureaucratic* norms use crystallized beliefs but with absolute standards. The good-performing organization is assessed by whether certain fixed targets are reached or not. *Expert* standards are generally comparative. The peer group operates as an institutional framework within which comparisons can take place, but the standards are essentially ambiguous. Finally, some standards involve ambiguous beliefs about absolute moral values; these are *ethical* standards. Morality knows no compromise and little comparison. To measure it and to define empirical standards is extremely difficult. Consequently, disputes over moral beliefs, such as in religious wars, become the most difficult to resolve.

This analysis of norms was tried out on the chief executives in our sample by asking them to rate the extent to which each of the four types of standards applied to their organization (see the Appendix). In this way, we tried to avoid the common complaint about typologies that organizations may display a mixture of types. Each organization thereby acquired a score for each of the four norm types.

These results were then factor analysed resulting in two clear dimensions which we call a *service norm* and an *efficiency norm* (see Figure 4.1). The service norm factor scores almost exclusively on the expert and moral standards, showing a negative relationship between the two. This indicates that our respondents tended to select one or the other of these measures. Similarly, the efficiency norm is heavily weighted towards the economic and bureaucratic characteristics, again showing

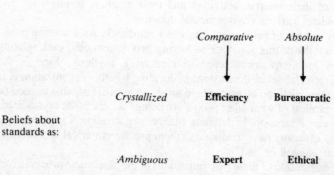

Figure 4.1 Types of norms

the strong negative relationship between the two norms. It appears that chief executives tended to choose one or the other norm to describe their organization.

Table 4.5 Factor analysis of 4 norm variables to give 2 norm factors

| | Norm factor | |
| | NMSE Service | NMEF Efficiency |
Norm variable		
Ethical: commitment to cause	−0.90	0.11
Expertise: service to client	0.80	0.06
Bureaucratic: smooth running with orderly procedures	0.13	−0.89
Efficiency: efficient use of resources	0.08	0.81
% variance	40.1	35.0
Eigen value	2.3	1.8

From these factor scores two new variables were created, the service and efficiency norms. Table 4.3 shows the results of the analysis of variance on standardized variables showing a significant difference in service norms across the five clusters at $p < 0.10$ with cluster CC showing the highest service score. These are the organizations pursuing multiple strategies which, as we have outlined, involves a considerable emphasis upon co-operative input and output strategies. We also note that this cluster is low on the efficiency norm. The low service norm cluster is cluster OC which also exhibits a low efficiency norm. These appear to be organizations in which the engine of strategy is to be found elsewhere. Norms do not constrain or promote strategy.

Context and strategy — a summary

Clusters and context

Contextual variables have been introduced individually whilst making some connections with strategy. We now attempt to pull these threads together into a coherent picture of possible connections between context and strategy. Table 4.6 summarizes the results of Table 4.3 in an attempt to provide an overall picture.

Variables of legacy income, operating uncertainty and variability, are omitted since the analysis shows they contribute no significant variance across clusters, or when contrasting cluster groupings. The two variables, reserves and service norm, which show some significant variance across all five cluster groups are rated as high (h), medium (m),

Table 4.6 Patterns of context and strategy

Contextual variable			Context		
	Dynamic 1	Dynamic 2	Service	Niche	Protected
Significant others	H	H	H	L	H
Giver dependence	H	H	H	L	H
Voluntary sector share	H	H	L	L	L
Voluntary sector share change	H	H	L	L	L
Income change	H	H	L	L	L
Covenant income	L	H	H	L	L
Reserves	M	M	L	M	H
Service norm	M	L	H	M	M
Efficiency norm	H	L	L	H	H
Strategy cluster	Extenders	Output co-operators	Competitive co-operators	Acquisitors	Reactors
	EX	OC	CC	AQ	RE
n	9	10	5	4	3

Notes: H = high
M = medium
L = low

and low (1). There is some arbitrariness in this since, ideally, we could justifiably use five categories but this would be at the expense of portraying an overall view. The remaining variables are rated high (h) and low (l) according to the particular cluster contrasts which are reported as significant (see Table 4.3).

Each overall context is summarized in Table 4.6. There are five contexts, Dynamic 1, Dynamic 2, Niche, Protected, and Service. Strategy clusters EX and OC are related to Dynamic 1 and 2 contexts, so labelled because both contexts score high on significant others, giver dependence, voluntary sector share, voluntary sector share change, and total income change. Dynamic contexts involve commensal awareness combined with high share and income growth. Both also have medium reserves. They differ only in that Dynamic 1 context is combined with low covenant income and a high efficiency norm, whereas Dynamic 2 includes the inverse of these two variables.

On the other side of Table 4.6 are two contrasting contexts, the Niche and Protected. The Niche context is characterized by low significant others, low giver dependence, low voluntary sector share, low voluntary sector share change, and low income share scores. The Protected context differs from this only in displaying high significant other and high reserve scores. The remaining context (service) can perhaps only be distinguished by a high service norm.

The combinations of context and strategy can be summarized as follows:

CONTEXT: Dynamic 1.
Many significant others, high voluntary sector share, income change. Efficiency norms.

STRATEGY: Extending (EX).
This is a specialized input-driven strategy seeking out new income opportunities and exploiting a natural growth in voluntary sector income.

Comments: This cluster is heavily populated with Third World secular organizations.
Strengths: Innovation and taking opportunities for expansion.
Weaknesses: May not do well in less expansive environment and have difficulty in coping with steady state conditions.

CONTEXT: Service.
High service norm and low reserves are the features of this context.

STRATEGY: Competitive co-operators (CC).
The service norm matches the client co-operation strategy which is the distinguishing feature of the strategy. This cluster tends to eschew extending or co-operating as regards inputs although it has slightly above average concern with input efficiency.

Comments: *Strengths*: The strengths of these organizations will be to develop close co-operative relationships with client and receiver groups.
Weaknesses: Their low profile on input extending could mean that they suffer from shortage of resources. The context suggests they are aware of significant others but they have less than average growth rate.

CONTEXT: Dynamic 2
A sub-type of dynamic 1. Many significant others, high voluntary sector share, share and income change. Distinguished from dynamic 1 by high covenant income and low service and efficiency norms.

STRATEGY: Output co-operators (OC).
This is an output driven strategy feeding off the available resources to create co-operative links with clients and receivers.

Comments: This cluster is heavily populated with Third World

Religious organizations and by some dominant well known national charities across all three industries. It is no criticism of them to say that they tend to wait for the resources to come to them whereas the extenders are more actively seeking inputs. Dynamics 1 and 2 together account for nineteen of the thirty-one organizations.

Strengths: Can develop a tremendous goodwill from clients.

Weaknesses: Emphasis upon client co-operation can lead to neglect of inputs.

CONTEXT: Niche.

Little concern for significant others. Below average voluntary sector share and income growth. Efficiency norms. All the signs of a self contained niche, medium reserves.

STRATEGY: Acquisitors (AQ).

This is an input efficiency driven strategy. Below average attempts to innovate and to co-operate on outputs since this is not required within the niche.

Comments: *Strengths*: These organizations concentrate upon doing what they already know but doing it better.

Weaknesses: The 'sticking to the knitting' approach may cause an in-built obsolescence which has happened to at least one organization in this cluster where their way of helping handicapped people has been superseded by changing technology.

CONTEXT: Protected.

This could be seen as a sub-type niche context but we see much concern for significant others and especially marked by very high reserves.

STRATEGY: Reactive (RE).

Since these organizations are sitting on a pile of gold they hardly have to do anything to gain more inputs. Hence a very low input extending score (see Table 3.4). They do score an intermediate level of output commensal co-operation.

Comments: There are only three organizations in this cluster. To a large extent this dilemma is a result of the concept of charity; since if people give to a cause, even if that cause declines in quantitative terms, the law does not allow the money to be used for other purposes.

Strengths: As long as the pot of gold lasts there is no problem.
Weaknesses: Reserves can run down. Perhaps more important in the long run, however, is the loss of legitimacy due to charities not using their resources to the public benefit.

Structure

Structure refers to the patterns of activities pursued by the participants of an organization. Here we are concerned with formal structure as representing the management blueprint of what is supposed to happen. Informal structure, the actual patterning, is a much more difficult feature to measure in an organization and was considered outside the scope of this project.

Formal structure starts with the organization chart although not all voluntary organizations necessarily acknowledge the existence of such a document. Nevertheless, managers may implicitly acknowledge a number of aspects of structure defining key areas such as who does what (specialization) , who reports to whom (span of control), the grouping of individuals (departmentalization), and the extent to which activities are defined in writing (formalization).

Explanations of structure

If formal structure represents a blueprint for organizational activities that blueprint could be expected to rest upon some strategic plan of campaign. Two broad explanations predominate in the organizational literature, the strategic and the contextual, and a third explanation assigns cause to other unspecified factors.

Strategy and structure

This explanation emanates particularly from the work of Chandler (1963) and his study of the development of the divisionalized structure of major American business corporations. An underlying thrust of this theory is that the divisionalized structure was developed to accommodate a greater range of product types and markets. Basing the departmentalization upon product lines, as in a divisionalized structure, made more sense than continuing with a functional structure in which departments are formed around process skills, because the management of the organization can more easily be oriented towards the marketplace requirements.

This line of argument has been more formally expressed through Williamson's (1976) notion of the M Form company (or the market form) in which the formation of product–market departments can be explained

67

in terms of transaction costs. In other words, as organizations developed more product lines and grew in size, often through vertical or horizontal integration, the complexities of managing the interdependencies within and between functions increased, thereby increasing managerial costs and giving an incentive to break the organization down into semi-autonomous product–market divisions. In this way, the large centralized headquarters staff could be reduced as each division developed its own staff expertise related to its own product–market conditions. Corporate headquarters now became, in Williamson's terms, a kind of internal capital market in which divisions would be competing for capital to finance their investment projects.

Context and structure

The contextual explanation for structure emanates from research in comparative organization theory particularly associated with the Aston Group (Pugh *et al.* 1969). The notion of context refers to the features of an organization and its environment that the management will take into account when determining structure. Internally this covers features such as technology and size, while externally it covers the major dependencies, uncertainty, and change.

Contextual variables include features such as size and technology. Another important variable was found to be dependence which is the extent to which an organization gains its resources from a relatively small number of sources and high dependence was found to increase centralization of decision making.

Other factors and structure

Although strategy and context have been shown to have a significant effect upon structure the fit is far from perfect. Another explanation for structure suggests that it may be an outcome of historical factors (Udy 1965), such as the era when an industry was founded. This argument is critical of the rational managerial explanations for structure, arguing that the degree of rationality in determining structure is quite small and the structures are more an outcome of habit or tradition.

This is not unrelated to an institutional explanation for organizational structures (Meyer and Rowan 1977) according to which public organizations in particular such as state schools have their structures determined for them by forces outside their own organizations. Hence one might say that the institutional environment, either by force of habit or tradition, or by dictate reduces the degree of managerial choice over structural dimensions. This institutional explanation of structure can be seen as rational in the sense that it reflects the rationality of an external force. However, we also might accept that there is a degree of randomness in the structure an organization takes and that within certain very broad limits the structure makes little or no difference to efficient operation.

The measurement of structure

Wherever possible structure was measured by means of established scales to assist comparison between our sample of organizations and other studies. In particular, the measures of specialization, formalization, and centralization as developed by Hickson *et al.* (1969) were used but adapted as appropriate for voluntary organizations.

Specialization is defined as the extent to which an organization employs people to carry out specific tasks. To measure this, an organization was assessed as to whether at least one person performed a particular task and no other task summed across nineteen different possible tasks. These range from the existence of people to deal only with accounts, fund raising, legal matters, training, etc.: see the Appendix for the full list.

Formalization is defined as the extent to which an organization writes down specific procedures and information. The items covered whether there was a written contract of employment, an organization chart available to a range of people, job descriptions, etc. (See the Appendix for the full list.)

Centralization is defined as the extent to which specific decisions are authorized high up in organizational hierarchy. The highest level was taken as above the chief executive (score 6) which occurs when a decision has to go to a board or to headquarters for authorization. Level 5 is for the chief executive authorization, down to level 1 as a field worker, or 0 as a collective decision by all members of the organization. There were twenty-eight specific decision topics, covering such matters as the decision to promote supervisory staff, to introduce a new method of fund raising, or to devise training methods (see Appendix A for the full list). Each decision topic was rated as to the level to which it would normally go and hence an overall centralization score could be achieved.

Span of control is defined as the number of people the chief executive has reporting directly to him or her.

Departmentalization is defined as the basis for grouping activities at a level below the chief executive. This was an aspect of structure not covered by the Aston gorup but it covers a major structural decision that has to be made in an organization. Simon (1956) identified four principal bases for departmentalization: by process, by product, by client, or by area. To these we add another two: by advisory staff function or by project. As Simon points out, however, these bases of departmentalization can overlap and hence the operationalization was devised in order to allow for degrees of a particular type of departmentalization. Any one organization therefore acquired a score as to the extent to which it had units reporting direct to the chief executive according to the above six categories.

The specific operationalization was carried out as follows:

Information was gathered from organization charts, chief executives, and other officials concerning which units reported directly to the chief executive whose predominant jobs covered the following categories:

Staff/advisory, i.e. non-workflow (personnel, administration, advertising).
Process, i.e. workflow but not a complete output/service and part of a wider operating process.
Product, i.e. workflow and producing good or service for delivery to clients and receivers.
Geographical area, i.e. region of country or world.
Client, i.e. a specified client as part of total clientele.
Project with a specific aim.

From these raw variables an adjusted score for each departmentalization type was computed to adjust for the size of the span of control of the CEO (see the Appendix for details of computation).

In order to discover any underlying dimensions of departmentalization the adjusted scores were factor analysed (Table 4.7). The factor loadings show a factor negatively related to staff/advisory departments but positively to product, area and client departments. This we call the divisional departmentalization variable variable (Dep 1). The other factor is loaded on the process and project variables which we call the functional departmentalization variable (Dep 2).

Table 4.7 Factor analysis of 6 departmentalization variables to give 2 factors

| | | Factor | |
| | | Divisional *Dep1* | Functional *Dep2* |
Factor	*Variable*		
Divisional:	Non-workflow staff	−0.80	−0.50
	Workflow, complete product	0.51	−0.12
	Geographical area	0.55	−0.32
	Client sub-group	0.58	0.08
Functional	Workflow, not complete product	−0.21	0.85
	Project	0.08	0.53
	% variance	26.6	22.4
	Eigen value	1.60	1.35

The interrelationships between the structure variables are shown by the Pearson correlation matrix in Table 4.8. From this we can see that specialization is strongly correlated with formalization and span, a finding that generally supports other studies using a similar methodology. Centralization appears quite independent of these variables and only a weak relationship ($r = -0.32$, $p < 0.10$) with functionalization providing a weak contradiction to the convention that functional organizations tend to be more centralized. We also note a weak relationship ($r = 0.32$, $p < 0.10$) between span and divisionalization, indicating that divisionalization is one but not the only way of coping with wider spans.

Table 4.8 Pearson's intercorrelations of structure variables

	1	2	3	4	5	6
1. Specialization	1	0.51*	0.03	0.50*	0.21	0.00
2. Formalization		1	0.05	0.17	0.11	−0.12
3. Centralization			1	−0.26	−0.10	−0.32†
4. Span				1	−0.32†	0.29
5. Divisionalization					1	0
6. Functionalization						1

Notes: $n = 31$
    * $p < 0.005$
    † $p < 0.10$

Structure, context, and strategy

We can now examine the possible relationship between structure, strategy, and context. Table 4.9 shows the means of each structure variable for each strategy cluster. We can see an almost completely random relationship between the two sets of variables except for some evidence that clusters EX and RE have lower functionalization scores than the other three clusters.

Table 4.9 Strategy cluster and structure

	Cluster					
	EX	CC	OC	AQ	RE	
Specialization	0.34	0.05	−0.23	−0.28	0.06	$p > 0.77$
Formalization	0.18	−0.30	0.01	−0.33	−0.08	$p > 0.95$
Centralization	0.30	0.22	−0.38	−0.30	0.40	$p > 0.53$
Span	−0.26	−0.25	0.22	0.03	0.51	$p > 0.73$
						1, 2 cf 3, 4, 5
Divisionalization	−0.07	0.31	−0.02	−0.12	−0.08	$p > 0.096$
Functionalization	−0.46	0.07	0.34	0.53	−0.44	$p > 0.33$
						1, 5 cf 2, 3, 4
						$p < 0.07$

Table 4.10 examines the relationships between structural variables and both context and the strategy variables (not clusters). Again, we note a paucity of significant Pearson's correlations. However, there are two significant correlations between voluntary sector share and specialization ($r = 0.64$, $p < 0.0001$) and formalization ($r = 0.44$, $p < 0.015$). If we take the voluntary sector as a surrogate for size as measured by number of participants we see confirmation of the familiar relationship between organizational size and these two structural variables.

The Pearson's correlations between the various structural, and contextual and strategic variables (Table 4.10) show a greater number of relationships between context and structure than between strategy and structure. To shed further light on this, two sets of multiple regressions were conducted both using structure as the dependent variables and using context and strategy as separate sets of independent variables.

Table 4.10 Pearson's correlations of structure, context, and strategy

	Spec.	Form.	Cent.	Span	Divi.	Func.
Contextual variables						
Dependence receiver	0.02	−0.02	0.02	0.08	0.06	0.43[b]
Dependence giver	0.11	0.18	0.11	0.03	−0.15	0.10
Voluntary sector share	0.64[a]	0.44[b]	−0.12	0.27	0.22	−0.08
Reserves	0.16	−0.13	−0.11	0.30	0.33[c]	−0.13
Income change	−0.19	0.21	−0.11	−0.20	0.10	0.08
Voluntary sector share change	−0.15	0.24	−0.06	−0.16	0.12	0.13
Service norm	0.30	0.30	0.01	0.25	0.13	0.15
Efficiency norm	−0.22	−0.38[c]	0.10	−0.30	−0.43[b]	−0.03
Operating uncertainty	0.07	0.00	−0.21	0.06	0.34[d]	−0.29
Strategy factor variables						
Input						
Extending	0.05	0.13	−0.07	−0.22	−0.12	−0.02
Co-operating	−0.11	0.04	0.20	−0.34[d]	0.00	−0.12
Efficiency	−0.10	−0.03	−0.12	−0.13	−0.08	−0.34[d]
Output						
Competition	0.22	0.12	0.09	−0.29	0.04	−0.18
Commensal co-operation	0.21	0.27	−0.09	0.15	0.05	−0.08
Client co-operation	−0.27	0.08	−0.11	−0.16	−0.18	0.09

Notes: a = $p < 0.0001$ b = $p < 0.02$ c = $p < 0.05$ d = $p < 0.10$

Table 4.11 shows the results for *context* where we can see that 56 per cent of the variance of specialization is explained by the contextual variables of voluntary sector share and income growth. Divisionalization is 46 per cent explained by receiver dependence, operating uncertainty, efficiency norm, and reserves with the latter as the most important variable.

Table 4.11 Structure and context

	Spec.	Form.	Cent.	Span	Divi.	Func.
			Structure variables			
Multiple R^2	0.56	0.34	0.21	0.21	0.46	0.37
Context						
Income growth	−0.32					
Voluntary sector share	**0.75**	**0.36**		**0.40**		
Dependence giver		0.28				
Dependence receiver					**0.29**	**0.33**
Operating uncertainty (1)					**0.33**	**−0.36**
Operating variability (2)						
Service norm (1)						
Efficiency norm (2)		**−0.35**			**−0.28**	
Reserves				0.28	0.35	
dt	2.25	3.24		2.24	4.22	2.24
F	16.01	4.04		3.24	4.76	4.45
b	0.00	0.02		0.05	0.01	0.02

Note: Bold denotes significance of < 0.05, otherwise < 0.15

When examining the effect of *strategy* variables upon structure we see very small amounts of variance explained. The results are given in Table 4.12. The relationship between strategy and context has also been explored by means of regression analysis and we see commensal co-operation (see Table 4.13) sharing 59 per cent of the variance explained. The −0.56 standardized regression coefficient indicates that commensal co-operation is reduced by voluntary sector share.

Table 4.12 Structure and strategy

	Spec.	Form.	Cent.	Span	Divi.	Func.
			Structure variables			
Multiple R^2	0.07	0.07	−	0.19	−	0.11
Strategy						
Input						
Extending	−	−		−	−	−
Co-operating	−	−		**−0.42**	−	−
Efficiency	−	−		−		**0.34**
Output						
Competition	−	−		−	−	−
Commensal Co-operation	−	0.27		0.28		−
Client Co-operation	−0.27	−		−		−
df	1.29	1.29		2.27		1.28
F	2.34	2.19		3.09		3.58
p	0.13	0.14		0.06		0.07

Note: Bold denotes a significicnce of < 0.05, otherwise < 0.15

Table 4.13 Strategy and context

	EXTN	Input COOP	EFFN	COMP	Output CPCM	CPCL
			Strategy factor variables			
Multiple R^2	0.17	–	0.18	0.17	0.59	0.24
Context						
Income growth	–		−0.28	–	**−0.56**	–
Voluntary sector share	–		–	–	–	–
Giver dependence	–		–		–	–
Receiver dependence	0.25		–	–	**−0.26**	–
Operating uncertainty	–		–	–	–	**−0.37**
Operating viability	–		–	0.41	–	–
Service norm	–		–	–	**0.41**	−0.24
Efficiency norm	–		–	–	**−0.30**	**−0.46**
Reserves	−0.29		**−0.43**	–	–	–
df	2.25	–	2.25	1.26	5.22	3.24
F	2.56	–	2.73	5.20	5.08	2.56
p	0.09	–	0.08	0.03	0.002	0.07

Note: Bold denotes significance level < 0.05, otherwise < 0.15

Lobbying

As already mentioned, lobbying is often an important part of an organization managing its environment. Table 4.14 shows the Pearson correlation coefficients between lobbying activity and lobbying co-operation for the contextual variables. From this we can see that lobbying activity is increased by both income growth ($r = 0.35$, $p < 0.06$), and voluntary share change ($r = 0.36$, $p < 0.06$), although the voluntary sector share shows no relationship with lobbying. Lobbying therefore appears as a

Table 4.14 Lobbying, context, and strategy: Pearson correlation coefficients

Contextual variable	Lobbying Activity LOBB	Lobbying Co-operation LOCO
Dependence receiver	−0.06	−0.22
Dependence giver	−0.12	−0.21
Voluntary sector share	0.03	−0.06
Reserves	−0.15	−0.45*
Total income change	0.35†	0.29
Voluntary sector share change	0.36†	0.28
Service norm	−0.03	0.07
Efficiency norm	−0.43*	0.01
Operating uncertainty	−0.04	−0.01
Operating variability	−0.05	−0.01

Notes: * $p < 0.02$
†$p < 0.06$

result of growth factors on the input side of the voluntary organization. We also note a strong negative relationship between norm 2 ($r = -0.43$, $p < 0.02$) and lobbying activity. Reserves also show a strong negative relationship with lobbying co-operation.

Referring back to the discussion of Tables 3.7 and 3.8 in the previous chapter, we noted a general lack of relationship between lobbying and strategy. We would here also have to accept a greater tendency for context rather than strategy to be affected by lobbying.

Summary

The purpose of this and the previous chapter has been to establish the principle of measuring organizational strategy and to relate strategy to organizational context. For this sample of voluntary organizations five strategy clusters have been evolved, the extender (EX), the competitive co-operative (CC), the output co-operative (OC), the acquisitive (AQ), and the reactive (RE).

There is some evidence to indicate that contextual factors are related to strategy. Specifically, the EX and OC strategies appear adapted to a more Dynamic context, while the AQ and RE strategies are more adapted to the Niche and Protected contexts while the CC strategy is adapted to the Service context.

Note

1. Again, the non-statistically minded reader may prefer to move to pp. 65–67 where the results of the following quantitative analysis are summarized.

Chapter five

Strategy cluster cases

This chapter gives a thumbnail sketch of each organization in our sample. The organizations are grouped under their respective strategic cluster (see Chapter 3) and the key elements of their strategic stances are outlined. The aim of these 'mini-cases' is to isolate and identify the prevailing themes of the strategic profile and to show in the case of each organization the specific ways in which they operate within the overall strategic cluster.

Strategy cluster EX: the extenders

Key strategic elements

All organizations in this cluster are characterized by a strategic profile which shows consistent and positive decision to extend both giver and client bases. The organizations which fall into this strategy cluster are shown in Table 5.1.

Oxfam (OXFA)

Aims since foundation forty and more years ago have been to relieve poverty, distress, and suffering in any part of the world. Oxfam is a large, well-known national organization which scores high on significant others (5 given, 8 received) showing a fair balance between others' awareness of it and its awareness of others in the sector. Output extending is seen in trying to change its image more to a developmental organization than an emergency organization. In delivering outputs it co-operates with virtually most of the other major Third World organizations hence deviating somewhat from the cluster norm of low receiver co-operation.

On the input side there is comparatively little emphasis on improving efficiency of known methods but innovation shows clearly in the attempt to develop more interaction with givers and up-dating the charity shops

Table 5.1 Organizations in the extender strategy cluster (EX)

Organization	Strategy characteristics
Oxfam	Well known in sector. Concerned with corporate image and achieving new methods of monetary input.
War on Want	Overtly political image. Seeking to extend more apolitical funding. Flexible almost modular provision of services.
Jewish Blind Society	Experimental and innovative in fund raising, especially through direct mail. Outputs modular and some routine in running day centres and homes.
Operation Road Runner	Aims for an output market niche – using large trucks to transport foodstuffs. Is looking to widen its funding base.
Guide Dogs for the Blind	Established, but still competes for funding and seeks to innovate in this area. Continually extending dog breeding and training methods.
London Association for the Blind	Actively seeking major changes in funding base. Is becoming increasingly specialized in provision of services. Aware of and adapting to change.
British Red Cross	Pursuing changes in funding base. Increasingly competitive rather than innovative towards outputs.
Voluntary Service Overseas	Actively trying to reduce dependence on government funding. Seeking to gain new receivers and new projects.
Royal London Society for the Blind	Actively trying to compete with larger organizations in the sector. Is trying to change corporate image and seeking to compete with state-run schools for the blind.

which are run as a separate arm of the organization. Surplus income from the shops is fed in for use in charitable activities. Oxfam is developing educational programmes in the UK to try to educate the public into Third World problems. Occasionally it lobbies government but generally without commensal co-operation although there is an increasing tendency to co-operate with other voluntary organizations for particular campaigns. Because of its widespread network both for inputs and outputs it is a divisionalized organization by geographical area with a wide average span of control (9) for its managers.

War on Want (WAWA)

Aims are to transfer wealth from Britain to the Third World and thereby to improve conditions in these countries. The organization delivers an overtly political message and it sees itself as primarily a development agency although it is one of the smaller organizations in the sector. These aims have not changed over thirty-five years.

War on Want sees itself as supported by a distinct group of supporters who display stronger political ideals than many supporters of other charities. Managers of War on Want are now trying to widen the giver base to increase independence (at present 15 per cent of funds come from EEC and other governmental sources). Presently the organization tends to have high giver and receiver dependence but this is coupled with a very fast growing income.

Managers are very aware of the sectoral field. Although small, War on Want has a high profile and is quite competitive towards extending on the output side. In particular, managers see the organization as in a battle with some US-based Third World agencies which are viewed as acting as an ideological arm of US government policy. War on Want scores above average for co-operation with receiver groups and is keen on evaluating those groups which it selects partly for what are considered appropriate political leanings. Operations are a mixture of *modular* in terms of having to adapt to new tasks and *routine* especially over the vetting of projects.

Organizational structure is simple, highly centralized, and has become more so as the current chief executive has tried to increase professionalization and to enforce the organization's political message. There has been a loss of collective decision making but more specialists have been introduced. The results of this strategy remain to be seen.

Jewish Blind Society (JWBS)

The aims of the organization are to help members of a particular religious persuasion, mainly elderly but some young, who are visually handicapped. It was founded over 160 years ago and runs residential homes and day centres. Its operations are a mixture of modular in respect of the social and some fund-raising activities, and routine for running day centres and fund raising.

There is evidence of high dependence upon givers with the biggest giver accounting for 15–20 per cent of income, and very dependent on receivers since residential homes absorb 45 per cent of expenditure.

This organization displays a very strong extending strategy towards inputs. Innovation is shown through experimenting with direct mail fund raising and trying to emphasize the need to reach a younger pool of visually handicapped. The organization also scores fairly high on the input efficiency factor thereby deviating somewhat from the cluster norm; although primacy must be given to its extending and innovating.

Operation Road Runner (OPRR)

This is the newest and smallest organization in the sample, only having started in 1985 initially with a grant from Oxfam to help the transportation of foodstuffs to Sudan and Ethiopia. The organization comprises a small enthusiastic team. One member has a great deal of international trucking experience. He was shocked by what he saw in the Middle East with well-known agencies not having the expertise to move food in bulk. The organization was especially critical of some unsuccessful attempts by Band Aid in this respect.

The strategic philosophy is highly innovative being based upon the concept of using very large super-trucks carrying up to 100 tons instead of using many smaller trucks. The organization scores very low on input co-operation. It is above the cluster average for output competition, trying very hard to make a mark for itself and sees itself as up against the 'big boys'. One of its main competitors is a German charity doing something similar. Road Runner scores no mentions received from other organizations in the sector but gives four. Generally very aware of the environment and of its sector.

Guide Dogs for the Blind Association (GDBA)

A large national charity with quite a high growth rate. The organization specializes in breeding and training dogs for the visually handicapped. In this sense it is continuing an innovation started more than fifty years ago but sees itself as innovating around this theme. Nevertheless, it is slightly below the cluster average for input extending and output competition, possibly reflecting its established position in its sector, but it does rate input efficiency somewhat higher than the cluster average. In particular, the chief executive emphasized the general competition for funding which was very high in this sector. The organization is regionally spread throughout the United Kingdom and the Chief Executive has a relatively wide span of control (10) very much like the Oxfam case.

London Association for the Blind (LAFB)

This organization, founded in the 1850s, caters for the visually handicapped by providing employment, teaching trade occupations, providing housing, and helping people with limited sight to read. The predominant operation is fairly routine as it runs holiday hotels, hostels, and homes. It is presently running at a deficit and is quite dependent (25 per cent) upon its largest giver, the local authorities. The organization has a factory which is run as a commercial operation.

For inputs managers are actively trying to extend to new givers and they have recently created a new information department to do this. Extending is also combined with efficiency, in this case to a greater extent than the cluster average and it is using work study to achieve this. At present it has very few co-operative input programmes, hence the organization scores below cluster average for input co-operation but it is considering moving in this direction. Income growth rate is low. Again, the chief executive views the input environment as highly competitive in this sector.

The output strategy shows a mixture of approaches, high on competition and efficiency but also co-operating in a number of ways. Commensal co-operation occurs with another visually handicapped organization (Royal National Institute for the Blind) and other co-operations include the Manpower Services Commission and a proposed co-operation with an Area Health Authority.

The organization has a greater lobbying profile than many voluntary organizations, specifically over issues of VAT reform. This involves co-operation with other charities (there is a charity VAT reform group of which it is a member) and the chief executive is personally active in lobbying government.

The development of a strategy is reflected in the increase in certain specialisms, specifically positions to control workflow, to acquire human resources, for training coupled with the appointment of an information officer. More formalized procedures have also been introduced, through specifying the chief executive's job more precisely. Decision making is quite centralized and the chief executive has a small span of control (4) in what is basically a functional organization structure. The moral norm was strongly emphasised. An operations committee has been formed along with a grants committee.

Changes in 'bought-in' skills have also been made to make the organization tighter and more professional. Specifically this has meant hiring new auditors, insurance brokers, and investment brokers.

Overall, London Association for the Blind is running as an increasingly tight organization, aware of a highly competitive environment. It only gave one mention of a significant other organization in the sector, but received eight mentions.

British Red Cross (BRRX)

This is an emergency relief organization founded 120 years ago specializing in medical problems which can happen anywhere in the world but which tend to be predominantly in the Third World. It has branches throughout the UK, runs a training/conference centre, and a home for the disabled. When operating overseas it emphasizes its political neutrality.

Traditionally it has been staffed by ex-military personnel but is now trying to professionalize. It is more aware of commensals (mentions given, five) than commensals are of it (mentions received, three).

Input strategies emphasize extending to new givers scoring very low on input efficiency concerns, probably reflecting the fairly high dependence upon government funds (20 per cent of total income from this source which is the biggest single giver) and a desire to try to break away from this. Hence it is actively pursuing new (for it) fund-raising devices such as payroll deduction and introducing a 'Friends' group. At the moment there is a heavy dependence upon legacy income (10 per cent) which it also wishes to break. Because of the importance of preserving a non-political stance the organization does little in the way of input co-operation with other organizations.

For outputs the organization is particularly stressing the improved efficiency of delivery rather than trying to reach out to new receivers. Since it operates in most countries of the world, it feels it cannot do much to increase significantly the client base. Services are delivered largely through commensal co-operation with established Third World charities such as Oxfam, CAFOD, and Save the Children Fund in programmes of short/medium duration and to some extent through central government's Overseas Development Association.

It sees increasing competition in the sector as leading to the need for more efficiency and it is also concerned to try to do more on the domestic front. Direct lobbying of government is definitely not considered feasible due to the need to maintain a non-political stance.

To implement its strategy specialist posts have been added for recruiting and training. The organization is at a mature stage of the life cycle, highly formalized, and relatively well specialized. The span of control of the chief executive is six (an increase of two over three years) and the departmentalization essentially reflects geographical operation. Recent years have seen an attempt to cope with and instigate change through increased professionalism.

Voluntary Service Overseas (VSO)

Founded over thirty years ago, the aims of this organization are to work for social and economic justice throughout the world and to build international friendship and understanding. It does this by recruiting people in the UK with a range of skills. They then spend a period in the Third World training and helping local people. It is, therefore, principally an educational organization operating (in July 1986) thirty-three projects overseas.

For a Third World Sector organization, it receives a very low significant others scores, receiving and giving only one meniton. It is highly dependent on one giver, the UK government, accounting for 85 per cent of its income and sees its task in a predominantly routine mode. It is, however, trying to break out of this mould and, hence, falls into our classification of strategic extenders.

For example, input strategy is broadly extending, trying to reach new givers, particularly by reducing dependence upon government funding and by seeking other institutional givers. Outputs show a fair degree of competition particularly in trying to extend to new clients.

The organization has traditionally been locked into a co-operative mode of strategy both on the input and output side, and it is currently trying to extend and work round this. There is still co-operation with other agencies such as Oxfam and Christian Aid for both inputs and the provision of services, but it is recognized that change must occur both to extend beyond this strategic mode and to begin to evaluate programme effectiveness.

Primarily, Voluntary Service Overseas is a functional organizational structure. The chief executive's span of control is six and overall formalization has increased over the last five or so years through the introduction of a manual of procedures for field workers and the new requirement for written reports. These latter are a result of the creation of a new managerial post to evaluate the effectiveness of programmes. Occasionally the organization lobbies government along with other agencies in the sector to press for more money for Third World causes.

Royal London Society for the Blind (RLSB)

The aims of the organization are to train and educate young visually handicapped people in order to prepare them for employment. In its present form, created seventy years ago (although with foundations going back 150 years), the aims have remained substantially unchanged although securing employment for the receivers now has a greater importance. It achieves this by running a training school. The organization also has a trading company which is a factory for making goods for sale. Expenditures are roughly equal between running workshops and the school.

Managers' awareness of significant other organizations in the sector is above average. This organization does not score high on input extending which is somewhat restricted due to its local domain and an agreement with Guide Dogs for the Blind which provides funds (hence high input co-operation). Its membership of this cluster is really justified by the high competition/extending for receivers, low input efficiency, and low output commensal co-operation. Also, as a small organization, it feels itself somewhat outpaced in new drives for funds, such as payroll giving, by what the chief executive called the 'biggies'. It is attempting to manage this by having businessmen on its Council. Dependence upon largest giver is small, accounting for 5 per cent of total income. It has a large number of single givers, the average donation being £9.

For receivers the organization is actively aware of having to compete with the state school system and local authority schools for the blind, especially as there is a trend to integrate visually handicapped children into state schools. The school accounts for 45 per cent of expenditure.

Operations of teaching and running workshops are an equal balance of routine and modular. Structure is fairly specialized but not formalized. It is essentially a functional organization structure with a chief executive's span of five.

The biggest strategic problem the organization is facing is the impact of the policy of community integration for visually handicapped and possibly a somewhat persistent Victorian image. However, this organization differs from the Reactors (to be described) in that its managers are aware of this and are trying to effect changes.

Summary of cluster EX: the extenders

Whilst each of the nine organizations in this cluster displays a number of characteristics which are particular to it (hence perhaps the commonly heard claim by many managers of voluntary organizations that their agency is unique) there is a very strong unifying theme in the recognition of environmental change and active strategic responses. The precise way in which each organization achieves this may differ: the similarities lie in the evident desire by their managers to experiment, innovate, and adopt the mantle of change both toward securing inputs and reducing dependence upon single givers (or a single mode of giving, such as legacies), and toward extending the type and range of services provided.

These are certainly the entrepreneurial organizations in our sample. They are organizations which are already undergoing a form of strategic renaissance or are organizations which have never settled down into any strategic niche. Their managers appear to seek the challenge of the future and are taking a proactive stance toward it.

Furthermore, such managers seem to have anticipated the need for change and have focussed their efforts not just on specific parts of the organization, but on its entirety, in particular balancing equally the need to sustain and develop both funding bases and service provision. There is also some evidence of increased professionalism either through the creation of new posts or by recruiting professional (non-charity based) managers.

Overall, all nine organizations display attempts at coherence. That is, not only is there evidence of organizational re-design in the form of increasing specialization or professionalization but also in the strategic positioning of the organization toward coping with or securing changes in the sector.

Strategy cluster CC: the competitive co-operators

Key strategic elements

All five organizations in this cluster compete and co-operate simultaneously in their sectors. Largely this is because they are operational (with the exception of Christian Aid) and cannot always provide a complete service on their own. Hence, they co-operate over service provision with other agencies. Competition for funds is fierce, however, and each organization displays a predominantly co-operative strategic profile toward securing inputs to maximize income. As a cluster the organizations have a high strategic profile overall, indicating a generally high level of managerial awareness for the need for proactive management and the adoption of strategies suited to the operational context of the organization. The organizations which comprise this strategy cluster are shown in Table 5.2.

Table 5.2 Organizations in the competitive co-operator strategy cluster (CC)

Organization	Strategy characteristics
British Leprosy Relief Association	Co-operates for income with Oxfam which is the largest source of funds. Joint ventures with Oxfam over service provision.
Sense	Long term co-operation for inputs with Royal National Institute for the Blind (RNIB). Co-operates with many other organizations in the sector for service provision.
International Christian Relief	A small operator in comparison with others in the cluster. Effectively a subsidiary of International Aid. Co-operates over service provision to many receivers, but principally operates in Ethiopia (currently).
Christian Aid	A prominent Third World religious charity. Partnerships with church bodies is the keynote strategic theme along with co-operation toward operational agencies overseas.
Royal Commonwealth Society for the Blind	Co-operates with other agencies and governments. Pools funds to build hospitals or provide services. Becoming more professionalized and will possibly become more competitive toward outputs over the next few years.

British Leprosy Relief Association (LEPRA)

Founded about sixty years ago, the aims of this organization are the treatment of a specific disease and education of the public about this. The organization has generally a low profile in the Third World sector. No other organizations in our sample mention LEPRA as a significant member of the sector.

For inputs it has moderate dependency upon the largest giver (Oxfam) which is very active in co-ordinating the efforts of voluntary organizations of many nations. It accounts for 18 per cent of total income.

Co-operation is LEPRA's principal strategy toward coping with this dependency. There is low income growth, and hence, within this context, innovating and extending is of less importance than co-operating in order to maintain the steady state.

For outputs commensal co-operation is very high, again reflecting joint activities with Oxfam. The organization does not engage in lobbying of any kind.

Operations are a balance between routine and modular. The introduction of a new drug required greater skill levels in the field, for instance, in the training of nurses. Specialization is at a moderate level but more significant is the creation of extra positions to cope with human resources management, control of workflow, and professionally to legitimize the organization. This is supported by the high expertise norm to describe organizational culture. The structure is a mixture of functional and geographical departmentalization.

Sense (SENS)

Founded over thirty years ago, the aims of this organization are to support the parents of visually handicapped children and to campaign on behalf of chidren whose senses are impaired as a result of the mother's illness from Rubella during pregnancy. Since a safe vaccine was introduced in 1970 the aim is to reach a 95 per cent immunization target. The organization is really a combination of self-help, an educational agency, and a pressure group.

On the one hand, Sense is a craft-based operation based upon residential services for adults and, on the other, it provides a modular educational family support activity. Sense also routinely organizes holidays. The organization's awareness profile in the sector is relatively low. It was only mentioned once by the other organizations in our sample.

The most important aspect of input strategy is long term co-operation with commensals, particularly with RNIB and local authorities since this is where half the income comes from. Other statutory bodies like the Manpower Services Commission and the Department of Health and Social Security also provide substantial income. The organization scores very high on input co-operation presumably in an attempt to sustain these stable funding relationships.

Sense's strategic profile toward service provision is equally characterized by co-operation. Especially high is commensal co-operation, a result of joining together with eleven other voluntary organizations in developing services, again including RNIB. Sense lobbies frequently for many purposes combining with other prominent commensals in the sector, thereby supporting their overall co-operative strategy.

International Christian Relief (ICHR)

This is a small Christian charity aiming to help the Third World persecuted. It is effectively a subsidiary of a larger charity, International Aid, and was founded ten years ago.

It is aware of many other organizations operating in the sector, but did not receive any mentions from organizations in our sample. Managers are aware of competition for resources but the organization is not particularly dependent upon any one giver. Similarly, dependence upon an individual receiver is very small but nearly one-quarter of its output is currently going to one country (Ethiopia). The organization is pursuing the high profile multiple strategies typical of this cluster with particular emphasis upon commensal and receiver co-operation for outputs and a co-operative strategy toward inputs. Lobbying is only done occasionally for the specific purpose of trying change VAT regulations through the VAT Reform Group.

The organization has a very simple structure with little specialization and formalization. Most decisions are made by the chief executive.

Christian Aid (CAID)

Founded forty-five years ago, this organization aims to combat malnutrition, disease, sickness, and distress throughout the world at the same time as purveying a broad Christian message. Four mentions given and six received from significant others in the sector so it is a prominent Third World charity. It is primarily a development and educational organization.

Overall, strategy emphasizes partnerships with other church bodies and with self-help groups indigenous to the receiver country. This is regarded as a more difficult task than solely sending money. Christian Aid's managers also view the environment as basically competitive both for funding where the organization competes with other church organizations and with new organizations entering the sector especially those from the United States. The organization also competes for receivers with these organizations. The actual tasks carried out are an almost equal mix of routine and modular.

Christian Aid collects 30 per cent of its funds through church sources, the biggest giver group, and 19 per cent from government grants, the second largest source. The effect of the new charities is beginning to be felt and even covenanted money through the church is a problem. There is a split between *fundamentalists*, the people who are more concerned with the after life, and the *social gospelites*, those interested in improving life on earth. Traditionally, giving to Christian Aid has come from the social gospelites but the fundamentalists are growing in strength which is perhaps reflected in a 40 per cent reduction in denominational giving between 1985 and 1986.

In response to the operating environment described above, Christian Aid's dominant strategic profile is one of co-operation with commensals, givers, and receivers (although the organization also competes quite heavily in outputs). One problem with this strategy, however, is its prodigious appetite for financial and human resources. Co-operating on such a large scale, especially with receiving agencies and indigenous groups, costs a lot of money. Very recently, moves are being made to reduce the amount of co-operation required whilst keeping the level of competition constant. Basically, this will mean concentrating upon relatively fewer receivers than before. Receivers will be assessed for their urgency of need or their congruency with Christian Aid's philosophy of helping the poor to help themselves. Those which meet these criteria will be funded. Those which do not, will receive a reduced level of funding or no funding at all.

Christian Aid does not lobby government. The organization is a matrix structure comprising functional and divisional departments or groups. There are growing concerns of increasing the level of professionalization, with a new personnel post already created, and management training beginning to occur. The chief executive has a current span of control of nine.

Royal Commonwealth Society for the Blind (RCSB)

This organization aims to combat blindness and to improve the independence and confidence of blind people, mainly in the Third World. It is primarily a treatment organization founded about forty years ago. It spans both the visually handicapped and Third World aid sectors with an emphasis on Bangladesh and Zimbabwe. RCSB also has an eye hospital at Bhopal in India. Managers gave two mentions of significant other organizations (one American and one Canadian eyecare organization) but received no mentions from the other organizations in our sample.

RCSB experiences the usual level of competition for inputs but tries to de-fuse output competition by explicit co-operation with other organizations. For inputs the organization is trying to diversify by attempting to increase the number of corporate givers, computerizing mailing lists, and trying to change the image of the organization from that of an old paternalistic colonial organization to a more modern and dynamic one. At the same time, RCSB is co-operating especially through relatively short-term programmes both with givers and commensals to secure inputs. RCSB pools money with other voluntary organizations to build, for example, a hospital or work with foreign governments which jointly carry out the task. It also has a number of shorter term co-operations with foreign governments and their agencies. British government agencies do not supply much in this way at all and RCSB is now trying to get more money out of EEC.

For outputs the organization is beginning to be less co-operative and is adopting a more highly competitive stance. In particular managers feel they must keep up with developments through new technologies of treatment and rehabilitation. RCSB is beginning to differentiate its strategy toward different countries. For instance, it has developed an alternative to Braille as a blind person's language based upon a number of different native languages. Similarly, a great deal of differential effort is going into training ophthalmologists in Africa where there is a great shortage. This shortage does not exist to the same extent in Asia.

Lobbying of the UK government never takes place but RCSB does occasionally lobby overseas governments in particular to sustain the education of children in school. This lobbying is often done in conjunction with other aid agencies.

Since a new director took over seven years ago the organization has developed a more precise and formalized structure. Specific posts added have been for fund raising, to develop administrative procedures and public relations and advertising. Formal procedures recently adopted have been a written policy description and written research reports. Centralization has also been increased.

A lot of emphasis has gone into changing the composition of the executive council which is effectively superior to the chief executive. The idea of the change is to abolish an 'old colonel' image and develop a more professional stance. The executive council could then become a decision-making unit not just something of a hindrance.

The span of control of the chief executive has increased in the last two to three years from 5 to 6. RCSB is mainly a divisionalized structure with four workflow divisions and two functional divisions reporting to the chief executive. Greater professionalization is reflected in the very high rating of the expertise norm in the organization.

Summary of cluster CC: the competitive co-operators

The reason for the dominantly co-operative strategic stance of these five organizations is perhaps found in their sector positioning. None of the five are sector leaders to the extent that they dominate the industry. They are, nevertheless, sizeable operators and thus gain significant advantages from co-operative strategies building internal strength from sharing risk and reducing operational uncertainty (Harrigan 1985, 1986, Pfeffer and Nowak 1976)

When it is advantageous, each of these organizations will compete. Yet not being a sector leader can result in reactive strategies being adopted to cope with changes in the industry as well as in operational demands. Managers thus seek a level of autonomy which co-operation can give. For three of the organizations (BLRA, SENS, and ICHR) co-operation appears to be an end in itself. Yet with Christian Aid and the Royal Commonwealth Society for the Blind, co-operative strategies seem to be rather more means to an end, in order to gain a secure enough footing to compete on an individual organizational basis. Success here would almost certainly bring with it less overt co-operation and would very likely shift these two organizations in cluster EX.

Strategy cluster OC: the output co-operators

Key strategic elements

This cluster comprises ten organizations and is probably the most diverse

Table 5.3 Organizations in the output co-operator strategy cluster (OC)

Organization	Strategy characteristics
Save the Children Fund	Demand for services very high. Non-routine task and seeks to make existing routes of funding more efficient rather than seek new avenues.
Royal Blind Asylum and School	Fairly routine inputs, over a third from local authorities. Very bland strategic profile overall with some commensal co-operation.
Action Aid	Single method of gaining funds (sponsorship). Highly co-operative strategy toward receivers.
Foster Parents' Plan	Co-operates on income via sponsorship programmes and equally strives for efficiency in securing income. Emphasizes co-operation with receivers.
World Vision	Primarily a fund-raising organization, the British division of a US-based child sponsorship charity. Sole receiver is the parent organization, hence co-operation.
Quaker Peace and Service	Emphasizes commensal and receiver co-operation. Tries to extend to new givers more than others in the cluster. Becoming more formalized and professionalized.
Catholic Agency for Overseas Development	Avoids direct competition by limiting its domain by supporters' faith. Engages in a number of co-operative joint ventures for outputs.
Royal National Institute for the Blind	A number of stable relationships with givers and many joint activities with schools, colleges and local authorities.
Water Aid	Linked into the Water Authorities and works closely with receivers co-operatively with governmental, other aid organizations, and some churches.
Bible Lands Society	Of all organizations in this cluster, this one is putting most recent effort into gaining new givers. Mostly characterized by its only high profile characteristic, receiver co-operation.

of all the clusters in terms of organizational type, size and sector position. The unifying themes of their strategic management are strongly oriented toward output co-operation either with organizations in the sector or with receivers (or both); a generally low overall strategic profile, but sufficiently oriented toward commensal and/or receiver co-operation to include them in the cluster.

Save the Children Fund (SCHF)

The aims are to protect children and see that they are given relief when required. It is still primarily an emergency relief organization although it is striving hard to move more towards development, treatment, and education. It is large and prominent in its sector, receiving ten mentions from other organizations but only gave the name of one significant other. The organization was founded more than seventy years ago.

The chief executive sees 'total competition' for inputs amongst other charities but sees plenty of demand for its services. The biggest single giver is the British government, accounting for 12 per cent of total funds. There is no particular identifiable single large receiver.

Managers see the organization's work as primarily non-routine in that emergencies cannot be predicted and 40 per cent of expenditure goes into this. A lot of work is also modular, involving intermediate treatment for young offenders in the UK (although primarily a Third World organization, approximately 14 per cent of expenditure is in the UK). SCHF also carries out some craft operations in running family centres and routine work running primary health care such as immunization and nutrition.

For inputs managers place great emphasis on efficiency rather than on extending by innovation. Input co-operation is also low. The picture here is of an organization that has secured plenty of resources and the main strategic problem is how to put them to good use. Hence we see a high score for output efficiency/extending and a fairly high score for receiver co-operation. SCHF occasionally lobbies the British government in conjunction with other large charities. It is mainly a functional organization with two geographical regions.

Royal Blind Asylum and School (RBAS)

This organization runs a school for the blind and a Braille press, taking roughly 46 per cent and 23 per cent respectively of expenditure; inputs include 35 per cent of total income from local authorities. The task involves largely a craft operation in running the school.

For inputs, efficiency is the main emphasis; there is little innovation. For outputs, there is some commensal co-operation with RNIB. RBAS occasionally lobbies government, particularly over matters such as the level of blind allowances given by the state.

Action Aid (ACTA)

The aims of this organization are poverty alleviation in Third World countries which it tries to achieve through the sponsorship of children. Managers gave six mentions of significant other organizations in the sector and received five. It is essentially based upon one method of gaining inputs and hence scores high on efficiency but low on extending/innovation and co-operation. For outputs ACTA scores highly on efficiency/extending, low on commensal co-operation, but high on receiver co-operation. This profile, based around extending the co-operative ventures with receivers, reflects the very specialized task of this organization.

Foster Parents' Plan (FOPP)

Aims are to improve the quality of the lives of children and families in the Third World and to foster genuine links and understanding across international boundaries. It is largely a development organization, founded in the late 1930s. The organization gives direct assistance to families through sponsorship, helps set up education programmes and community development. The organization operates wholly in the Third World. Respondents mentioned no significant other organizations in this sector, but received two mentions from others in our sample.

The educational side of organization requires a flexible (modular) operating core whereas giving primary health care is fairly routine. In securing inputs managers rate efficiency very high but also stress co-operation through sponsorship programmes. Sponsorship involves very close links between the organization and the sponsor. For outputs the dominant strategy is toward receiver co-operation.

World Vision (WVIS)

This is the British arm of a large international American child sponsorship charity and its aim is to raise money to send to the parent organization. It is primarily a fund-raising organization, operations being mainly a routine clerical job. Spending decisions are made in the United States although the chief executive of WVIS has a say in this. The organization also has evangelical aims. Monies are entirely spent in the Third World.

Respondents mentioned fifteen significant other organizations in the sector (the highest of any organization in the sample) and received six mentions from other organizations, also well above the Third World average of 2.24 due mainly to some arguably controversial aspects of its operation. In the financial year 1985–6, the biggest single giver was Band Aid, accounting for 20 per cent of total income.

In securing income, the organization emphasizes efficiency and co-operation through child sponsorship where a giver undertakes to 'adopt' a child in the Third World. For outputs, the organization's receiver is the parent organization. This is reflected in the organization's highly co-operative strategy. WVIS is sometimes seen as brash and over-sentimental in its approach by some of its British rivals in the sector but this may be envy of its success.

The emphasis toward an input efficiency strategy is reflected in organizational changes. Positions have recently been added for the control of obtaining materials, for accounting, and for recruiting voluntary workers. Formalization has also increased through adding information booklets, a formal organization chart, and work schedules.

Quaker Peace and Service (QUPS)

This religious Third World organization was founded over 100 years ago. Respondents gave four mentions of significant others in the sector and received five from organizations in our sample. Strategic aims emphasize the bringing of peace as well as the alleviation of suffering. QUPS puts these into practice through the education of receivers and disseminating information to a wider public. Hence, the most important task is to change attitudes (a modular operation), then to work for peace in the UK (a craft operation), and then as a comparatively routine operation the application of loans for practical projects. QUPS attempts to work through diplomats in trying to press for peace in conflict areas. Hence a lot of its work is defined as 'learning, meeting people, and persuasion'.

The biggest single giver, as with most of the religious charities which are arms of churches, is the parent church itself, but QUPS also received £1.2 million of its annual income in 1986 from the business community.

The primary input strategy is extending. Managers are very aware of a narrow giver base and are trying to widen this through advertising and increasing the number of corporate givers. Output strategies emphasize commensal and receiver co-operation which are the basis of this strategy cluster. QUPS co-operates with the National Church Council of Kenya, Botswana Refugee Council, British Council of Churches, British Refugee Council, CND, and Amnesty International. It also sees lobbying government as a vital part of its output, doing it in indirect ways, however, by putting diplomats in touch with one another.

Organizational structure is based upon eight geographical areas and has eighty full-time staff but it is comparatively unspecialized and unformalized. One of the major problems facing the organization is the need to recruit and train young people and for this purpose a training position has been added. There is also increased formalization taking place through the documentation of a formal organization chart and manuals of procedure.

Catholic Agency for Overseas Development (CAFOD)

The organization was founded twenty-five years ago as a Third World religious agency for funding emergency and development projects overseas. Managers recognize four other significant organizations in the sector, CAFOD, however, has a special constituency (according their supporters' faith) and it tries to avoid direct competition. The largest single giver is the Overseas Development Agency of the British government, accounting for 8 per cent of total income. Outputs are dispersed to seventy countries. Each project is evaluated by a committee and managers view this as primarily a modular type of task but also one involving a considerable amount of routine work.

For inputs, CAFOD is trying to develop some co-operative efforts, for instance, covenanting, and to improve its existing proven methods of gaining resources. It is not an innovator. For outputs, strategy is characterized by the emphasized development of a range of co-operative ventures. CAFOD is very insistent that there is no competition with other major agencies. Co-operation covers links with a number of religious bodies and committees in Europe and the development of long-term, three-year programmes in Africa. The organization emphasizes that it does not just want a financial relationship. CAFOD occasionally lobbies for more favourable terms from government in conjunction with other aid organizations.

The organization is fairly small (approximately fifty full time staff) and unspecialized and non-formalized. Ethical norms are emphasized above all others. The chief executive's span of control is 6, having increased by 2 in the last three years. Departmentalization is roughly balanced between functional and divisional.

Royal National Institute for the Blind (RNIB)

This is a large national charity in the visually handicapped industry. RNIB has broad aims, namely to educate, train, and rehabilitate the blind and other visually handicapped people, to promote research, and to educate the public. At its foundation (100 years ago) it was a self-help group, but now it has developmental, informational, and educational activities. RNIB has a high level of awareness in the visually handicapped sector. No less than eight other organizations in our sample mentioned it as a significant operator in the industry.

For inputs RNIB competes primarily with Guide Dogs for the Blind (cluster 1). RNIB is, however, a non-extending organization for inputs scoring highest on input co-operation strategy and about average on efficiency. At 32 per cent of total income, various forms of government funding constitute the biggest single giver. The organization has a number of stable relationships with other givers.

Although over the years there have been some innovations, for outputs it scores low on efficiency/innovation since the stock of blind people is fairly constant. The main output strategy is co-operation and here there are many joint activities. These include the running of a number of schools, colleges, and resource centres in conjunction with local authorities or other organizations. There are also links with universities for research purposes. RNIB runs a trading company. It is also very active in pressuring government to change the law to enable technicians, rather than surgeons, to remove eyes from the dead to try to increase levels of supply.

Its operations are substantially routine (covering the production of Braille books and tape services), but also include a high proportion of craft (for teaching) and non-routine (for teaching maladjusted as well as visually handicapped).

Strategy is changing, recently, particularly following the appointment of a young chief executive from outside RNIB and the organization is now considering a wide range of issues by carrying out demographic studies (see RNIB case study, Chapter 6). RNIB is constantly lobbying government and there is now a full-time parliamentary officer to do this. Lobbying is usually done in conjunction with other organizations.

As a large voluntary organization (1,400 full time staff) it is already highly specialized although some new positions have been created in the past two to three years. These are to recruit/co-ordinate voluntary workers, to develop and operate administrative procedures, for training and for market research.

The chief executive's span of control (11) is relatively large. The organization is structured along mainly functional lines but also has three divisions responsible for a 'product' line (i.e. for a complete output). Norms are reported as equally balanced between moral, expert, and bureaucratic.

Water Aid (WATA)

This is a comparatively new charity founded about six years ago to supply safe water and sanitation, and to support related self-help initiatives in the Third World. It is a development organization of a very specific type and is currently operating on two continents.

As this organization is linked in with the water industry it has an assured income base with potential access to a very large constituency. The original idea was an innovation but once that had been acted upon no further innovation was required. Hence, for inputs this organization scores below average for extending and for co-operation.

The uniqueness of WATA's position has meant little competition for funds so far. The organization obtains funds from water industry employees by payroll deductions and a voluntary effort from within the industry. But as growth occurs managers see the need to widen the base of support and are now approaching consumers (on a trial basis) via water bills. Here they are aware of the danger of poaching other givers, but take the view that because of the specific nature of their task, this danger will not be realized. The feeling is that existing established large Third World charities are not doing enough for water projects and, hence, they feel they have a role to play.

On the output side, this organization scores high on receiver co-operation but low on commensal co-operation. In order to carry out water projects, WATA works closely with governmental and aid organizations in the recipient country. These partnerships also often include churches. For example, in Ghana they link with the Presbyterian and Roman Catholic Churches, in Sierra Leone with the Water Supply Division of the Ministry of Energy. There is such demand for water projects that competition for receivers is irrelevant. In any case, competition is presently avoided by the large degree of collaboration with other organizations. However, managers see the possibility occurring in the future of competition for good projects.

At present, the largest single receiver is the government of Sierra Leone (10 per cent of expenditure), followed by the Presbyterian Church of Ghana. WATA managers are very insistent upon developing sound evaluation procedures for projects. Many governments request cash help but WATA encourages self help. This means that instead of direct cash requests, applications are made and supported by detailed plans. Thus the initial expectations of potential receivers may be disappointed but in the end the self-help approach is considered to be the best since receivers come to appreciate the technical expertise which WATA can offer.

The task of the organization involves giving advice and direct practical help. Projects vary greatly in relation to the problems presented as each village has its own requirements but the means of achieving them are usually clear. Hence the bulk of operations are modular. But there is also a considerable element of operational routine in processing applications.

With thirty-five full-time employees (fifteen in the UK) the organization is very simple, non-specialized, and non-formal. The chief executive has a span of control of three, one accountant, one UK operations and one overseas manager. It has yet to resolve the problem of to whom senior field engineers report and the degree of autonomy they have. These people are experienced water engineers who work for about forty days per year for WATA.

Bible Lands Society (BLSO)

This is primarily a Third World sector organization although it is involved in visually handicapped work. Its aims are to assist Christian missions to relieve pain and suffering, heal the sick, care for the poor, blind, crippled, and mentally handicapped children in lands of the Bible. Although originally a missionary organization, it is now an aid to missions. There is no active development work. The blind have always been a client for BLSO but it is only recently that the mentally and physically handicapped have been catered for.

The organization began as a Mission Aid Society in Turkey 130 years ago but the real foundation of the present-day organization can be traced back to the Second World War. The pressure which shaped organization strategy came from a group of young soldiers and chaplains who had been stationed in the Middle East. When they returned, they were concerned to find a charity in the UK which could help the blind, and to a lesser extent those with leprosy. The society had been in decline for some years, so its council were happy to hand over to these soldiers, who effectively ran the organization.

Gradually, the blind and lepers became a less pressing problem (a declining market) so, in the 1950s and 1960s BLSO began giving aid to mentally and physically handicapped. The organization still retains one school (Helen Keller House) for the blind in Jerusalem — but nowadays the ethos is *not* to keep blind children separate but to integrate them into the school system. Helen Keller House will continue but will not expand.

Respondents mentioned seven significant other organizations in the sector but received no mentions from others in our sample. BLSO managers are aware of a number of new organizations entering the Third World aid field particularly through child sponsorship. US organizations were mentioned specifically, and BLSO now operates such a sponsorship scheme. For this there is competition. For inputs the organization experiences general competition for an overall charitable purse. Traditionally it has relied upon a large number of individuals who did not enquire too closely as to how funds were spent. Now they are increasingly aware of the need to attract younger givers. Hence for input strategies we see a fairly high extending strategy (high for this cluster) since the organization is now putting a lot of effort into this. Payroll deduction is being pursued and so is the development of the 'Friends of BLSO' scheme. Advertising expenditure quadrupled from 1984 to 1985. The trading company is the biggest single source of income (30–40 per cent). This not only sells Christmas cards and associated goods but individuals also enclose donations with orders. The next biggest source of income is covenants and legacies. Givers still generally do not question where the money goes. Initially it was thought that Band Aid would reduce their overall income but this has not happened.

For outputs, co-operation with receivers is the only high profile factor.

This usually means a mission or an overseas group of helpers/developers to whom BLSO give money. The organization prefers to keep a stable receiver group in this way. The largest single set of receivers is in Lebanon and Syria which accounts for 40 per cent of expenditure.

The primary task is collecting and giving money. It is thus a fairly routine operation although the issues involved can vary. The organization also operates on a modular basis which covers more directly operational matters such as aiding the blind and lepers. The organization does not lobby government.

It is a small organization of eighteen full-time staff. Specialization and formalization is very low although some specialist positions covering finance, employment, and a secretary have recently been added and so have formal job descriptions. The chief executive's span of control is 17 with responsibilities assigned primarily on a complete product/service basis. It is accepted that there has been a tension for change in the organization, since for thirty years it had been run by one person (hence the span of 17) but a new chief executive appointed from outside the voluntary sector is currently trying to achieve significant changes in strategy and structure.

Summary of cluster OC: the output co-operators

This is a very diverse cluster. The feature in common amongst the organizations is that their predominant output strategy is either commensal or receiver co-operation, or both. Apart from two organizations they all score low on input extending. These two exceptions (QUPS and BLSO) are both missionary organizations with low growth, of different religious persuasions but aware of the need to break out of a rut. All the other organizations have relatively assured inputs. For them, acquiring funds is not the key problem so they actively pursue output strategies instead. This view is also supported by the high rating on efficiency for all organizations except for QUPS and BLSO mentioned above. It is not that these organizations are devoid of an input strategy but that they are emphasizing doing what is known to them better as far as raising funds is concerned.

It is also notable that a number of the organizations in this cluster have relatively long histories (such as RNIB and Bible Lands Society) whilst others are very much newcomers (Water Aid, World Vision). In this diversity, however, lies a unifying theme of activating or planning for change. For those organizations which have operated along broadly similar lines for a number of years the impetus for change is readily explained. In the newer organizations, the propensity toward output co-operation is viewed by managers to result ultimately in stagnation as service provision becomes institutionalized (see Water Aid, for example). Thus, the impetus for change is really an avoidance strategy against the danger of the organization becoming quickly locked into inter-organizational networks and arrangements. The case study of the Royal National Institute for the Blind (see Chapter 6) details the factors which are driving strategic change processes in this established organization. In doing this, the case is aimed at exemplifying the underlying dynamic of the whole cluster. Given the increasing harshness of today's operating environment it is doubtful whether an organization which was strategically oriented solely toward output co-operation would survive for long.

Strategy cluster AQ: the acquisitors

Key strategic elements

All the four organizations in this cluster are characterized by their emphasis upon securing input efficiency. Equally, they may be characterized by a generally low level of either innovating or extending strategies. The organizations are shown in Table 5.4.

Table 5.4 Organizations in the acquisitor strategy cluster (AQ)

Organization	Strategy characteristics
Unicef	All operations are directly accountable to International Headquarters in US. One aim of the organization is essentially for fund raising, whilst the other deals with giving direct aid to children in need.
British Wireless for the Blind	The organization is supported by a long-term fixed set of givers. Since only one appeal per year is allowed there are severe limits upon pursuing a strategy other than input efficiency.
Royal National Lifeboat Institution	Almost unique in the services it provides. Can be viewed as a voluntary substitute for what would otherwise be a governmental task. For givers, RNLI is really the only choice of organization in sea rescue. RNLI has no real need to compete for outputs, so concentrates on input efficiency instead.
Greater London Fund for the Blind	Essentially a fund-raising organization. Outputs are directed at other charities which have stable and formal arrangements with the organization. There is no rationale in strategically pursuing any option other than increasing the efficiency of inputs.

Unicef (UNIC)

This organization gives direct assistance to children in need mainly overseas. It also attempts to raise the awareness of people in the UK concerning such problems in other countries. These aims, since its foundation forty years ago, have increasingly stressed this advocacy role. Respondents viewed the organization as unique (it has greater scope than most), mentioning only one significant other organization in the industry. This view of its own uniqueness is apparently shared by other charities since it received no mentions from other organizations in our sample.

There is a high level of competition for inputs and this is reflected in the high input efficiency strategy score. As part of this, the development of mailing lists, Christmas card sales and the like have been implemented. The largest givers are foreign governments, in particular the US government (10 per cent) and the Italian government (10 per cent). Girl Guides also contributed a similar amount. Extending/innovating scores are low but co-operative programmes with givers (not commensals) are a major source of funding (e.g. through a schools' programme) and covenanting is also encouraged. There is also a move to increase advertising expenditure but this needs Board approval (in USA). Co-operation is also sought through bodies like the National Council for Voluntary Organizations for lobbying government over issues such as VAT. Advocacy is carried out by lobbying and also through the schools' programme.

Since all money goes to the International Headquarters, there is hardly any active pursuit of an output strategy. Headquarters are in the USA and the chief executive of Unicef has no say in how money is spent.

It is a small organization with little specialization and formalization. The chief executive's span of control has reduced from 8 to 3 over the past three years. There is one functional (non workflow administration) position, and two workflow complete service positions reporting to chief executive, one covering fund raising and the other information and advocacy. This organization has therefore linked its internal functional areas directly to its two major tasks.

British Wireless for the Blind (BRWS)

Founded in the late 1920s, the aims of this organization are to ensure that 'all registered blind people over the age of 16 years who are in need of a radio may have one'. It is, therefore, primarily an alleviation organization although it also provides advice to recipients (or their carers) on how to use audio equipment. It is an independent organization but previously it was a subsidiary of a larger visually handicapped charity (RNIB) and it still rents a room in its building. BRWS serves a specific niche. Respondents mentioned one significant other organization in the industry but received no mentions from other organizations in our sample. Its biggest single giver (British Forces Broadcasting Service) accounts for 40 per cent of total income.

For input strategies the organization primarily stresses efficiency in acquiring funds from an existing set of givers and, second, some extension to new givers. The extent to which this can be effective however is limited by the organization's Charter which only allows one appeal per year. BRWS can, however, advertise in legal journals and journals for the blind. Sixty per cent of people giving to BRWS go to a solicitor first. Co-operative relationships exist between BRWS and the British Forces Overseas who have adopted them as 'their' charity.

The organization has a very low profile of output strategies, although there are some. Innovations are being considered; the use of audio tapes and computers in particular. There is some commensal co-operation with a number of agencies, particularly social services departments. Co-operative strategies are not pursued with receivers to any great extent. The organization does no lobbying of government.

The central organization is small, employing six full-time people although there are part-time staff in over 200 agencies throughout the UK. The emphasis upon achieving efficiency in both input and output strategy is organizationally reflected by the addition of specialists for accounting and for administrative procedures. The structure is primarily functional with a span of control of 3 for the chief executive.

Royal National Lifeboat Institution (RNLI)

Founded about 160 years ago with the aim of saving life at sea, this is one of the most prominent British charities. Originally nearer to a self-help organization in so far as it consisted of fishermen helping themselves when they got into difficulty, it expanded to include other sea-going vessels and more recently to assist the growing number of leisure boat owners who get themselves into difficulties on the water. RNLI operates 200 lifeboat stations through the British Isles (UK and Ireland).

Managers view RNLI as being in strong competition for inputs. When there is a marine disaster people give generously but there is a tendency to forget them in quiet times (see Chapter 6). Input strategy emphasizes efficiency especially through advertising. Overall, strategy scores low on extending/innovating. The organization is unusual in that it receives a large proportion (almost 50 per cent) of its income from legacies. Twenty-five to thirty per cent of income comes from individual donations. There is no government money. RNLI is now adopting a more aggressive stance toward givers.

Output strategy, in common with three out of the four organizations in this cluster, emphasizes commensal co-operation. The links it forms with other organizations are vital, especially with the RAF and Coastguards, in carrying out rescues. RNLI sees its duty to rescue anyone in peril on the sea but obviously very little in the way of long-term receiver co-operation can be sensibly achieved, hence there is a low score on this strategy factor. In the past unsuccessful attempts have been made to develop co-operation with merchant seamen where rescues from commercially owned vessels are made. Over recent years expenditure on rescuing fishermen and commercial vessels has reduced as a proportion of overall expenditure as more resources are spent on private pleasure rescues.

The importance of other organizational linkages is not fully reflected in the strategy factor scores. Not only are the operational linkages with the RAF and the Coastguard vital, but more institutional links with the Ministry of Defence, Department of Trade, and the Home Office are also important. There are additionally some linkages with the Department of Health and Social Security. Since the late nineteenth century, when it was first suggested that RNLI might be nationalized (a suggestion which still arises every so often) an important part of overall strategy has been to manage the institutional environment through these linkages. RNLI is also the co-ordinating body for other lifeboat organizations in forty countries throughout the world. These are organized under the umbrella of the International Lifeboat Federation, for which RNLI provides the secretariat.

The main operations involve running 200 Lifeboat stations. This is rated as a modular task (i.e. there is variability in the task faced during rescuing but the means are relatively well defined). There is also a lot of routine work especially in both boat maintenance and administrative procedures.

An average station has 15 people (with a range from 3 to 30) including 9 (range 5 to 12) administrative staff. Mechanics and engineers are paid full time and the coxswain paid a retainer. The crew otherwise is voluntary. There are 2,000 fund-raising branches which operate as groups of volunteers. In addition to the rescue programme, 20–25 per cent expenditure is allocated for building new lifeboats. Presently this is running at 30 per cent, but this is unusually high. RNLI lobbies government occasionally especially over VAT which creates a problem, since much of its expenditure is on VAT-rated goods. This lobbying is done in conjunction with other charities.

As a large voluntary organization (630 full-time staff) it is highly specialized and formalized. The chief executive's span of control is 16, having increased from 10 in the past three years. It is essentially functionally organized. The strategy of this organization is detailed as a case study in Chapter 6.

Greater London Fund for the Blind (GLFB)

The aims of this organization are to act as a fund-raising organization for the visually handicapped and to pass these funds on to a committee consisting of sixteen charities. The organization was founded sixty-five years ago.

Strategy follows the cluster pattern of emphasizing input efficiency strategy. The organization does this through organizing the well-tried methods of postal appeals and social events although it has also innovated some new fund-raising measures. Outputs are entirely dictated by agreement with the receiving member charities with which GLFB has stable and formalized relations. For this organization, receivers and commensals are the same and so the output strategy is positive on both these factors.

The RNIB is the largest receiver (18 per cent of expenditure). Accountability is high since the chief executive must present financial statements to the controlling committee. As a fund-raising organization the task is very routine. Occasionally, GLFB lobbies government through the Charities' VAT reform group. There are forty-six full-time staff. Specialization and formalization are low and are not increasing. It is essentially a functional organization with a span of control of 6 for the chief executive.

Summary of cluster AQ: the acquisitors

The consistent pattern in these organizations' strategic profile is that either they are locked into inter-organizational networks essentially as a fund-raising arm of a larger charitable whole (Unicef, GLFB) or they are virtually unique in their domain (RNLI, BRWS). This makes concentration on securing input efficiency of primary concern, since receivers provide little in the way of competitive threat. In the case of RNLI, there is literally no alternative organization to carry out sea rescue and it would be equally difficult to find a precise substitute for British Wireless for the Blind.

These factors make the management of these organizations somewhat less ambiguous than those in the preceding three clusters. Correspondingly, appropriate organizational structures become more apparent, since a functional design caters for the majority of organizational concerns leaving only a small amount of other tasks to be accommodated into the structure. Strategically, the concentration upon efficiency in securing inputs makes sense although changes in the sector of operations (the industry) could imply a drastic strategic re-think. Such organizations really need to build into their structures and processes contingency plans for dealing with future changes. This is simply because even a small swing in context (from a change in input sourcing to a change in client base) will render the current set of strategies wholly inappropriate. The organization may be efficient, but it could equally well go efficiently out of business.

Building in the capacity to handle future change will, of course, take a number of resources from current operations but for organizations the size of RNLI and Unicef this should present little problem. It is the smaller organizations, such as British Wireless for the Blind and Greater London Society for the Blind, which will find building in spare capacity difficult. If RNIB were to move into the market currently served by British Wireless for the Blind, it is difficult to foresee how the smaller organization could continue to operate.

The message for these organizations would seem to be not to take their market niche for granted and, along with securing efficiency in inputs, concentrate upon developing and widening the niche they have secured.

Strategy cluster RE: the reactors

Key strategic elements

The three organizations in this cluster are characterized by their general lack of any predominant strategic profile whatsoever. Two of the three organizations seem content to accept their fate in the face of a diminishing market. Both these organizations fall into the visually handicapped industry. The other organization, Methodist Relief and Development Fund, appears less resigned to its strategic fate at the hands of the market, although it can hardly be said to be strategically proactive in the Third World overseas aid industry. It has a profile characterized by security in its domain. The organization is locked into a ready-made set of partners and sources of finance.

Table 5.5 Organizations in the reactor strategy cluster (RE)

Organization	Strategy characteristics
Methodist Relief and Development Fund	Run by one of the major churches with much money coming from covenants. A small organization with a relatively fixed set of receivers to whom it gives funds.
St Dunstan's	Originally set up to cater for war blinded ex-servicemen, the organization faces a declining market. Little attempts are visible to turn the organization away from what would appear to be inevitable further decline and eventual demise.
Scottish Institute for the War Blinded	Caters for the war blinded in Scotland. Heavily dependent on legacies and locked into a small set of givers and receivers. Insular, with little strategic effort to develop or change.

Methodist Relief and Development Fund (MRDF)

The aims of this organization are the relief, rehabilitation, development, and education of people in the Third World. It is run by one of the major churches. The original organization, the Methodist Relief Foundation, was founded in the 1930s, but the present Methodist Relief and Development Fund was formed in 1985 through a merger between the Methodist Relief Fund and The World Development Fund. The task involves assessing requests and administering funds which are given as grants. This is essentially a routine technology although there is also an equal degree of less routine modular technology which involves more active decision-making.

As a member of a large church group, which is its principal source of income, MRDF does not compete for inputs with peer organizations. It does not look further for funds. Similarly, MRDF does not compete for receivers. Input strategy is therefore low on input extending, input efficiency, and output competition. There is a feeling amongst respondents that the organization needs to extend itself, find new methods, or improve existing methods of gaining funds. It has recently acquired a large grant from the EEC, although this is viewed as unrepresentative. The giver base is large, over 8,000 churches and a lot of income is derived from covenants.

A feature of this organization (which distinguishes it from the others in the cluster) is its very marked co-operative strategy towards inputs. This is in part a function of supporting specific projects through sponsorship by individual churches. MRDF also co-operates with another Christian-based voluntary organization for advice but not for funds.

The major output strategy is co-operation, although managers see lobbying as an important part of their strategy. The organization has taken part in the Brandt lobby, pressuring Western governments to spend more on aid. It is a very small organization with hardly any specialization.

St Dunstan's (STDS)

The organization helps people who are visually handicapped as a result of war. STDS runs homes, provides training and rehabilitation, helps people settle into employment, and funds research projects. This is mainly a modular type of technology. Other aspects, however, such as skill training involve tasks which are more precisely a craft technology.

The organization is unusual. Almost no efforts are made to acquire new funds and the constituency of receivers is shrinking. Forty per cent of income comes from investments (it has very large reserves) and 50 per cent from legacies. The organization neither extends nor increases efficiency and hardly co-operates (apart from with some regular givers).

For receivers the organization does not compete but, nevertheless, there is a concern to reach out to new beneficiaries who are eligible. It also co-operates with commensals (GDBA and RNIB) for advice and belongs to a joint committee concerned with helping blind ex-servicemen. Because of the decline in numbers of war blinded ex-servicemen, managers envisage possible closure of the organization at some point in the future.

There is a medium level of specialization. It is the only organization in the sample to lose a functional position (buying). The chief executive has a span of control of 10. It is primarily a five-product line organization with two welfare officers, an industrial and research officer, a pensions officer and a hobbies and workshops manager.

Scottish Institute for the War Blinded (SIWB)

Aims are to help the war blinded and visually handicapped and centred in one region of the UK. Founded in 1915, the organization does this through education and training for which it runs workshops (taking 26 per cent of annual expenditure). Technology is seen as equally routine and modular. Welfare of receivers accounts for 58 per cent of expenditure. Respondents mentioned one significant other organization in the sector.

For outputs there is little competition for funds since fund raising is confined to its region. Legacies account for 50 per cent of income and rents and investments 28 per cent (in 1985). As for St Dunstan's (which it closely resembles), input strategy is low on all three factors. There is no attempt to extend the giving or to increase efficiency of existing methods. It does enter into joint programmes with some givers, hence, the input co-operation factor is not the lowest for the sample.

For its size, the organization is specialized and formalized but no changes in these have occurred in the last two to three years. The span of control of the chief executive is 16 and departmentalization is mainly functional. Overall this organization has an identical pattern of input strategy factors. For outputs it shows a wholly reactive stance.

Summary of cluster RE: the reactors

As Miles and Snow (1978) point out, reactivity is a way of surviving which can be suited to particular conditions. For STDS and SIWB these are conditions largely outside their control in the sense that the population of war blind is declining. Indeed, one could argue that this is a fortunate position for any charity to find itself in since it means that the original cause for its foundation had been eradicated. Reactive strategies, however, would appear to be less justified in cases where there is manifestly still a major problem to be solved as in the case of Third World aid.

The analysis so far has proceeded upon the basis of being able to establish certain strategic profile groupings of organizations (see Table 5.6). Membership of each group, or cluster, is determined by the score of each organization upon the basic strategic variables. Clusters are useful

Table 5.6 Strategy clusters: strategy factors (16 variables − >6 factors)

	Input strategic factors			Output strategic factors		
	Extending	Co-operation	Efficiency	Competition	Commensal co-operation	Receiver co-operation
OXFA	1.20	−0.09	−1.13	0.31	0.00	−0.16
WAWA	1.50	0.38	−1.50	0.27	−1.28	0.32
JWBS	1.85	−0.03	0.17	0.32	−1.07	−0.29
OPRR	0.64	−1.10	−0.17	1.28	−1.31	−0.53
GDBA	0.79	−1.14	−0.07	0.18	−0.27	−0.78
LAFB	0.63	−1.06	−0.38	0.50	−0.02	0.03
BRRX	0.58	−1.30	−1.70	−0.19	0.25	−1.47
VSO	0.57	1.46	−1.39	0.28	−0.09	0.53
RLSB	−0.04	1.00	−1.20	0.79	−1.03	−0.01
Cluster mean	**0.86**	**−0.21**	**−0.82**	**0.42**	**−0.60**	**−0.26**
BLRA	0.55	0.83	−0.53	0.29	2.08	0.14
SENS	−0.47	0.77	−0.17	0.20	1.28	−0.35
ICHR	0.50	0.72	−0.19	1.57	0.75	0.79
CAID	0.19	1.21	1.17	1.43	0.77	0.70
RCSB	1.12	1.56	1.66	1.44	1.32	−0.75
Cluster mean	**0.38**	**1.02**	**0.39**	**0.99**	**1.24**	**0.10**
SCHF	0.06	−0.74	0.71	0.62	−0.25	0.03
RBAS	−0.41	−0.66	0.53	−0.05	0.01	−0.07
ACTA	−1.13	−0.75	0.75	1.19	−0.02	1.17
FOPP	−0.73	1.18	1.18	0.23	−0.90	1.63
WVIS	−0.13	0.14	0.15	−0.70	−0.20	1.89
QUPS	0.77	−0.12	−0.33	−0.46	0.63	1.02
CAFO	−0.22	0.81	0.53	−0.60	0.19	0.42
RNIB	−0.53	0.36	0.03	−1.79	0.83	1.06
WATA	−0.00	−1.18	0.15	−0.35	−2.07	1.05
BLSO	0.44	−1.12	−0.42	−1.50	−0.27	0.79
Cluster mean	**−0.19**	**−0.21**	**0.33**	**−0.34**	**−0.21**	**0.90**
UNIC	−0.64	0.99	1.25	−1.51	−1.61	−1.73
BRWS	−0.35	−0.52	1.35	0.27	0.18	−2.01
RNLI	−0.41	−0.85	1.60	−0.41	0.56	−1.72
GLFB	0.15	−1.52	1.43	−2.89	0.44	0.18
Cluster mean	**−0.31**	**−0.48**	**1.41**	**−1.13**	**0.11**	**−1.32**
MRDF	−1.39	2.05	−0.91	−0.81	1.96	−0.14
STDS	−2.63	−0.72	−1.34	0.43	0.55	−0.01
SIWB	−2.46	−0.58	−1.24	−0.38	−0.58	−1.72
Cluster mean	**−2.16**	**0.25**	**−1.16**	**−0.25**	**0.57**	**−0.62**

for drawing generalized conclusions about the types of strategies pursued by organizations but within each cluster no two organizations will be identical. Hence, clusters are a way of finding similarities between groups of organizations but can also be used to distinguish differences between individual organizations within each cluster.

The purpose of this chapter has been to highlight the similarities and differences within each cluster. Perhaps one over-riding impression created by this description has been the variety of specific actions that organizations can take in order to achieve viability within their environments. A central theme to our methodology has been to combine the generalizability achievable from a wider sample survey with the in-depth textual analysis that can be provided by a case study method. The 'mini-cases' above are a step in this direction but, in addition to these, we present four more detailed case studies, each of which enables greater attention to the process of strategy formulation and change than hitherto possible. These cases are now to be presented in Chapter 6. The original criterion was to have one case study from each cluster as a representative of that cluster. Due to practical problems of data collection we were not able to complete our case study for an organization in cluster 1. All other clusters are represented.

The cases are: Christian Aid (cluster CC — the competitive co-operators), Royal National Institute for the Blind (cluster OC — the output co-operators), Royal National Lifeboat Institution (cluster AQ — the acquisitors), and St Dunstan's (cluster RE — the reactors).

Chapter six

The descriptive cases

Case study 1: Christian Aid. A competitive co-operator

Introduction

This case is designed to illustrate the opportunities and difficulties presented by a rather established and, as we shall see, traditional charity in the process of fairly radical structural and strategic change. The case is thus a slice out of recent organizational history and as a result the genesis and early days of Christian Aid are not covered in detail. Suffice it to say that Christian Aid is a child of the British Council of Churches (and in turn a member of the World Council of Churches based in Geneva). Since its foundation forty-five years ago, Christian Aid has experienced growth almost non-stop to a point where some of its members consider it very much a case of a child which has outgrown its parent! Nevertheless, Christian Aid remains a division of the British Council of Churches. The aims of the organization are to combat disease, malnutrition, distress, and sickness throughout the world and to effect this within the aegis of a broad Christian message. The organization comprises almost 200 staff with 130 of these based at headquarters in London and some 70 based at Area offices around the UK.

The changes in Christian Aid

In April 1986, Christian Aid changed its structure from a centralized, hierarchical bureaucracy to a decentralized matrix (or web) structure. What initially appears to be an overnight change in fact had its roots in tensions and difficulties which had begun to develop under two previous directors, Kenneth Slack and Charles Elliot. Some six months were spent researching Christian Aid collecting data on the nature and implications of this change and some of the issues which arose from this extended study are reported here. Since many of the data are confidential, a full account is precluded. However, the processes of strategic and structural change outlined in this case throw a great deal of light on the questions of managing such change processes.

Under Kenneth Slack and Charles Elliot, the organization had experienced growth and development. Particularly under the former director, Christian Aid had experienced a rapid expansion of its services and of its income. At the time of Kenneth Slack's directorship, the income for Christian Aid was around £5 million. Today it is around £17 million. Its major services comprise working through the churches and related agencies in Third World countries and financing these with a view to relieving the root causes of the problems. Christian Aid is not itself a development agency. It acts as the financier of other agencies in the field (which sometimes includes indigenous groups rather than church agencies) under the guiding maxim of 'helping the poor to help themselves'. The constancy of this strategic commitment is notable, for it has persisted through a number of other fundamental changes, including the recent massive structural reorganization. In order to be effective, Christian Aid views its purpose as helping the poor to become strong enough for them to fight against the factors which keep them in poverty. In other words, Christian Aid tries to make the poor more proactive so that they are in a position to fight hunger, provide education to their children, earn their own living, and plan for their own future.

It is hardly surprising, therefore, to discover that the original structure of Christian Aid was a centralized, functionally differentiated bureaucracy, controlled by a large board. Functionally, there was a marked emphasis toward aid, and grant making, as a department. Other departments included education, fundraising and so on, but the strategic emphasis within the organization was upon aid. Indeed, the majority of the board members at this time only had experience of grant making and other aid department issues. Board members were relatively inexperienced in other areas of organizational activity.

As the organization grew and the tasks it took on became greater and more complex, regional committees were set up to deal with specific nations. Asia/Pacific, Africa/Middle East and Latin/Central America were formed in 1975. Although this catered for the increasing complexity facing Christian Aid, it created some fundamental internal tensions and problems which were to be the touchstone of future problems and ultimately the impetus for radical reorganization. One of these tensions lay in the composition and power of the board itself. Not only were the board members disproportionately oriented toward aid, they also retained the power of veto over all suggestions coming from the new committees. Thus, if proposals did not fit into board policy they could be rejected.

Christian Aid was now by any definition a complex organization and the suggestion by the board that all problems emanating from the organization could be labelled aid issues was becoming questioned. Many functions (the education department, for example) felt that their terrain was either being ignored or poorly represented at board level. Since education at this time were also reponsible for the total organization of the annual Christian Aid Week, the major source of income in any one year (see Table 6.1), they felt justified in claiming some autonomy from the aid department and the direct influence of the board.

Table 6.1 Main sources of income for Christian Aid (£s)

Source	1986	1987
Christian Aid Week	5,684,929	5,869,000
Donations	1,983,242	1,906,000
Special appeals	2,643,115	2,174,000
Harvest income	96,980	108,000
Other donations	1,983,242	1,906,000
Covenants	1,400,563	1,548,000
Legacies	1,115,601	1,301,000
Government grants to specific projects	3,242,351	2,797,000
Other Income (includes investment and sales of assets)	997,435	1,054,000

The increasing complexity and size of Christian Aid was also causing some problems for its then director, Charles Elliot. He had been an effective leader of the organization whilst it was relatively small. He proved less effective as the organization grew and the task of director became less personal and more managerial. This was to result in his resignation. Essentially removing himself from any active management tasks, Elliot succeeded in reaffirming the primacy of the aid department, increasing resentment of this and excessive centralization elsewhere in the organization. It also emphasized the divisions between practising Christians and non-practising Christians on the staff.

Although Christian Aid is a division of the British Council of Churches and is in our classification a religious Third World organization, it does employ non-practising Christians on its staff. Quite naturally, differences of opinion over the organization's goals and modes of operation exist between these groups of employees (as they do between practising Christians themselves) and there are usually arenas in the organization where these can be debated or integrated. The absence of Elliot and the subsequent lack of any firm control or direction exacerbated these differences and also led to the suspicion among many employees that really what was happening in the organization was a struggle for strategic supremacy by the functions and that it was going to be an 'aid take-over'.

The current head of aid at this time recognized these feelings throughout the organization. His response was to let the department drift along with no clear leadership and no clear strategy. At this point, Christian Aid became almost wholly without clear goals or future strategy. Charles Elliot had virtually left Christian Aid, leaving it with no one at the helm.

An options group, convened largely through the suggestions of the head of education, began looking at the possibility of adopting a more participative and democratic organizational structure. The aim was to find a structure which would allow responsible autonomy and decentralization. All functions and departments should participate in decision making. In conjunction with the internal recommendations which were beginning to emerge, an external consultant was also asked to comment upon the possible reorganization of Christian Aid and his report was submitted to the board. Sir Brian Young (chairman of the board) read the report and asked Mary Applebey (a board member) to take a look at the recommendations suggested. Ultimately, the Applebey Committee was formed. This group examined the consultant's recommendations. Their aim was:

To relieve the director of decisional authority on virtually every issue.
To release creative energy in the staff.
To increase the level and efficacy of communication amongst all staff.

The consultant's report suggested the adoption of a matrix structure. This was in line with what many individuals in the organization had been thinking. There had been preferences suggested for a more 'network' kind of structure, involving everyone, in which decision making could be more participative. However, the matrix structure suggested was a much more extreme form of organizational structure. It was perhaps this extremity which caused the organization some problems in both changing structure and in implementing the matrix.

The external consultant suggested a structure in which an organization of consent could be achieved. Decisions should be achieved by asking staff to comment on and complete tasks, rather than telling them or using hierarchical power. The Applebey Committee took this suggestion to heart and the structure depicted in Chapter 2 (Figure 2.3) was the result. It was implemented in April 1986.

The essential features of the workings of this structure can be outlined. Each department which dealt with a specific geographical area, such as Africa/Middle East, was to form one arm of the matrix. The other arms were to intersect the geographical areas and these comprised the functional departments such as aid, education, communication, finance, and fund raising. The intention was to have representation of these functional sectors in each of the regional groups through a system of core and associate members. Core members were those who were permanent members of a regional group and were involved in all decisions therein, whilst associate members were less involved directly in the day-to-day affairs of the group. The primary forum in which all groups and sectors were to be represented was the strategic management team (SMT). Heads of sectors and groups met together under this banner to discuss issues arising from the various operational areas of the organization and to debate policy issues and strategic decisions emanating from the directorate.

The intention was that the whole organization should be structurally a single matrix. Charles Elliot had left the organization and a temporary acting director was installed pending the appointment of a new director. During this time, the matrix structure was implemented. One assurance was that despite the degree of change this was to bring about, no one was to lose their job and no one was to be downgraded. In fact, the adoption of the matrix resulted in a significant expansion of the organization and new jobs were created.

At the time of the change, problems began to surface almost immediately across the organization as a whole and within various groups and sectors. One obvious issue was that some groups and sectors found it easier to adapt to the new structure than others. For some, it required less of a radical change. Africa/Middle East, for example, took on the mantle of the matrix without experiencing much difference in its core activities, while the education sector could see no place for them in the matrix at all and experienced great difficulties in adapting to it. Overall, the matrix suited the overseas regional groups to a greater extent than the sectors which generally found difficulty in adapting to their new roles.

In particular, the structural change was difficult for two parts of the organization. Education (a sector) experienced a great deal of difficulty in adapting to the demands of the matrix and its stance was to refuse to be a part of it. UK/Ireland (a regional group) also seemed to fit badly into the adopted structure. Neither group or sector was against the new structure *per se*. It was rather that it could not see how its current tasks fitted into, or could be improved by, the adoption of a matrix structure.

Both these examples reflect Christian Aid's duality of strategic commitment toward givers as well as receivers which virtually all charities face to some degree (see Chapter 2). In Christian Aid, the adoption of a matrix structure was congruent with the strategies and interests of the overseas groups who provide services to receivers, but was at odds with the two areas which provided services to the givers (UK/Ireland and Education). Both these departments work closely with area staff in the UK in order to get a coherent programme of support and dissemination of information about the organization.

In this, they are specialists since they do not deal with specific geographical areas. UK/Ireland, for example, specializes in maintaining relationships with the churches at a national level and with area staff at a more local level. The department is designed to keep information about Christian Aid flowing to the constituent churches and to create and maintain this network. Education similarly is designed to get the message of Christian Aid's activities across to individuals in the UK who are already or might become givers (schools, youth clubs, etc).

During this time, a new director, Reverend Michael Taylor, was appointed. The stated brief for his job was to continue and to develop the matrix structure. Education's resistance was strong enough for it to be effectively excluded from the matrix and three new posts in education were recruited, one each in the overseas groups. These new posts relate primarily to their overseas group and hardly at all to the central tasks of the educational sector. UK/Ireland group was included in the matrix, but was to sit somewhat unhappily in the organization alongside the overseas groups whose tasks are far more focussed and less ambiguous.

Apart from highlighting the tensions between strategic orientation toward givers and receivers, the adoption of a matrix structure also highlighted a number of operating problems in the organization. This became especially true in regard to strategic decision making.

Organizational strategy and structural change

Whilst the adoption of the matrix structure was remarkable for its speed of implementation, it did not follow to the letter all the recommendations proposed in the consultant's report and the Applebey Committee. Notable differences in practice were:

1. There was not meant to be the post of associate director. Even if the role tasks of this post were to be retained, the position was to be re-titled since it was argued to carry with it undesired connotations of centralization. However, the post was retained and is still called associate director.
2. All the organization was to become part of the matrix. In fact, not all parts of the organization have been fully accommodated into the structure (such as education) so the structure in practice is something of a hybrid rather than a full matrix.
3. The original plan was not to have a separate UK/Ireland group since

the three overseas groups already had domestic responsibilities. On his appointment, however, Michael Taylor emphasized the strategic nature of the UK/Ireland orientation, in particular for sustaining a domestic constituency through contact with the churches at both national and regional levels. At the same time, a new department (fund raising) was formed in order to sustain the new and vigorous effort which was being mobilized to increase the organization's funding base.

4. Staff in the regional areas of UK were initially going to be attached to headquarters through the overseas regional groups. In practice, all area secretaries are part of UK/Ireland.

In other respects, the matrix corresponds with the blueprints originally laid down. One of the key aspects of this design concerned the organization of strategic decision making which was to be concentrated in a new forum, the Strategic Management Team (SMT), in which all groups and sectors are represented. In theory, this provides a participative forum for decisions to be discussed and action taken. In practice, this design too has proved something of a problem for Christian Aid.

One reason is that SMT rapidly became the focus of virtually all issues in the organization, irrespective of their strategic or operational orientation. As many respondents noted, SMT became something of a 'plug' in the organizational communication system. Since there was also a lack of effective feedback mechanisms from SMT to the rest of the organization (minutes were unclear and in shorthand so it was often unclear even what was under discussion), decision-making processes soon became bogged down. Simply too much information and too many issues came through SMT.

At the same time, the organization was undergoing quite substantial strategic changes in connection with its service provision. Christian Aid's traditional way of operating was to have no staff of its own overseas but to work in tandem with ecumenical bodies in various countries. Very little sorting of funding priorities occurred. Following the installation of Michael Taylor, the strategic mission of the organization became less ambiguous toward service provision.

The stated aim of the organization was to strengthen the poor rather than just relieve them. This brought with it two implications. One was that to achieve this aim efforts had to be directed at not just relieving poverty but to mobilizing and actively strengthening the weak to look after themselves. In many repects, this is similar to the strategic shifts in Oxfam (described earlier in this book) toward attacking the causes, rather than the manifestations, of poverty. A second implication for Christian Aid was that, for the first time, it would have to be relatively selective over where funding was allocated, guided by questions such as 'who is the weaker of these two' cases, for example, or 'might it be useful not to fund at present and think of other ways of giving aid?'

The perceived image of the organization thus became crucial since the constituency of givers can raise questions over possible selective funding or of increased autonomy to Christan Aid's overseas ecumenical partners. The role of the newly created UK/Ireland group is central here, since part of its activities is to keep trustees and funding bodies satisfied over issues of service provision. Certainly, questions of ideological or political discrimination should not arise.

These changes in strategy and structure have concentrated strategic issues at the level of SMT in the organization. Not only does the problem of too many issues arise, but also the role of SMT is not explicitly clear. For example, it is neither an executive body which makes decisions and then tells the rest of the organization, nor is it a forum which reaches recommendations over issues and then tries to sell them to the other parts of the organization. Respondents consistently indicated that the matrix structure itself was welcome. It increased participation and allowed the development of personal freedom in the the job. On the other hand, it concentrated authority in the hands of individual representatives from groups and sectors who sat on SMT.

Problems have begun to emerge as a result of using this system of decision making. Achieving consensus in decision making is more difficult. Whilst it is recognized that achieving full consensus on all issues is an unrealistic ideal, it is still felt that any other system of reaching a decision (such as voting) is inconsistent with the culture of this religious charity. SMT is forced to operate on a system of voting or averaging given the complexity of its task.

Respondents indicated that when individuals are overruled or outvoted in Christian Aid, they feel that they are being judged on their moral or ethical feelings and beliefs. So being outvoted, which is common practice in commercial organizations, is very uncomfortable for some members of this charity. Associated concerns are that in order to ensure full debate and participation on all issues, the amount of paperwork created and the levels of debate which are reached become dysfunctional. Some respondents indicated that the matrix structure had also caused decision making to be 'inward looking'. That is, SMT was considered to be the appropriate forum for all issues. The use of outside experts or other consultative bodies was not necessary since the organization had become 'self sufficient' in this regard.

In the process of working with Christian Aid, the authors of this book saw the potential for organizing decision making in an alternative way. Broadly, decisions could be categorized as policy issues (the statements about future direction of the organization), strategic issues (the alternative ways of achieving policies), and operating decisions (day-to-day issues and general system support decisions). Both policy and operating decisions should be taken out of the direct attention of SMT and delegated elsewhere in the organization, leaving SMT to concentrate upon strategic issues. Of course, there would still have to be interplay between policy and strategy and the director would still have to consult with SMT, but ultimate responsibility for policy would lie with the director.

To what extent Christian Aid follows this kind of route remains to be seen. What is important for research purposes is that changes in the strategy and structure of Christian Aid brought with them a number of central problems which were difficult to predict. They are also problems which are not unique to this organization. We shall see in the later case studies and in the organizations from the wider sample that similar issues arise. Common themes emerge over questions of organizational design, the role of management and management style, achieving participation and responsible autonomy at the same time as striving for strategic coherence. These are issues which virtually all charitable organizations are currently facing and they represent possibly the largest challenge so far to effective and efficient management.

Case study 2: Royal National Insitute for the Blind (RNIB). An output co-operator

Introduction

RNIB was founded by Dr Thomas Rhodes Armitage in 1868. Armitage was a physician who was unable to continue his medical practice due to failing eyesight. His decision to help fellow sufferers resulted in the large and well known organization the Royal National Institute for the Blind. For two years Armitage visited blind persons for whom he found that provision outside family help was almost non-existent. Many were beggars. He was convinced that blind people needed independence, and that this could be achieved through education and vocational training.

Some schools already existed to help the blind, but they were badly resourced, had no agreed way of learning to read by touch, and offered no after-care services at all. Armitage set up an executive council of blind men to evaluate the kinds of embossed type which were available and this resulted in the adoption of Braille as the standard for touch reading. Its adaptability into any language and into music and formulae is well known today. The organization was called the British and Foreign Society for Improving the Embossed Literature of the Blind and its first efforts were to introduce Braille.

In 1914, the organization became known as the National Institute for the Blind (NIB) and in 1918 the first school was opened. This was a

Sunshine Nursery School for the pre-school blind. This was followed by the Chorleywood College for girls, in 1921, and Worcester College, in 1937. Many other schools have been opened since, some specializing in caring for the additional physical and mental handicaps which blind people sometimes suffer. Rushton Hall and Condover Hall are examples. The Chairman of NIB, Captain Sir Beachcroft Towse, himself blinded after the Boer War, opened up his own home as a rehabilitation centre which was the first of many initiatives in this direction.

The organization was granted a Royal Charter in 1949 and it became the Royal National Institute for the Blind in 1953. Since then, the organization has diversified into a large number of supporting activities for the blind which include the provision of commercial college and a National Eye Donor Scheme (1962).

Strategy and change in RNIB

For over 100 years, the dominant strategy of RNIB was one of steady and incremental growth. As a result, the organization developed many stable inter-organizational relationships, especially with schools, colleges, and government agencies. In our classification of strategies, RNIB falls into cluster three, the output co-operators.

From the early days of Rhodes Armitage, the organization expanded its activities to encompass a wide range of services directly or indirectly to the blind. Examples of this are talking books, aids and games, and extensive information services. Initially, the organization had been set up for the sole purpose of promoting the use of Braille and from these beginnings it has grown into an organization with 1,700 paid employees and an annual turnover of £25 million.

The first indications of the changes in strategy which were to take place can be traced back approximately to the tenure of Eric Boulter as director-general in the early 1970s. At this time, the organization had evolved as the primary national voluntary agency for dealing with the visually handicapped and was substantially supported by government funds. It was felt by many individuals in RNIB, at this time, that the core financial input to the visually handicapped *should* come from government sources and that RNIB's task should be to allocate and administer such funds. Thus, efforts put into fund raising were minimal particularly in comparison to the advances made in this respect by other charities such as Oxfam and Save the Children Fund.

Two separate events led to the initiation of strategic change. First, Boulter felt that the services provided by the organization were not always congruent with the changing and often complex needs of the visually handicapped. He therefore introduced visually handicapped people into the management committee to a far greater extent than had previously been the case. Second, the country as a whole and the voluntary sector in particular suffered from the economic recession of the 1970s. The recession hit RNIB hard. It brought with it the realization that government funding was not necessarily going to continue at its present levels and, indeed, the spirit of the times was rapidly becoming one of questioning the role and the domain of the Welfare State and heralded a trend toward individualism and self-help in the financing of voluntary organizations.

The visually handicapped members of the management committee confirmed to Boulter that many of the services currently provided by RNIB did not necessarily take into account the needs of the visually handicapped community. In particular, there was a general feeling that RNIB should become more involved at the local and grassroots level rather than remain a distant provider or facilitator of services.

Whilst the seeds of change were sown, putting these into effect was another matter. For one thing the context of the recession meant that resources were scarce. RNIB certainly did not have enough money to manage large-scale strategic change in the the services it provided. At this time, the organizational structure comprised six divisions, and complex differentiation also served as barrier to effecting change since there was little integration between divisions. This structure is shown in Figure 6.1 and its role in hampering change is discussed in a later section of this case study.

Immediately following these two pressures for change, there was some fine tuning of services provided to the visually handicapped, although there were no significant efforts to raise funds from alternative sources. Strategically, the organization reacted to the immediate pressures of the needs of the visually handicapped. Managers were, however, ignoring issues of future funding profiles, the management of change to accommodate these, and the identification of future strategies which would establish the pattern of RNIB's activities in the voluntary sector, and which would support the further provision of services to the visually handicapped.

During the late 1970s, Boulter left RNIB and was replaced by Eddie Venn as director-general. The organization had emerged from the stringencies of the recession in better shape than many of its sister charities. One key reason for this was that the organization relied very heavily upon income from legacies (almost 50 per cent of income was generated in this way).

The effects of the recession had been to cause inflation, which was most memorably reflected in a significant increase in house prices. Thus, legacies became more valuable in real terms, as individuals with estates had both more disposable income as well as having proportionately more money to leave to charity. Nevertheless, managers in RNIB still had not

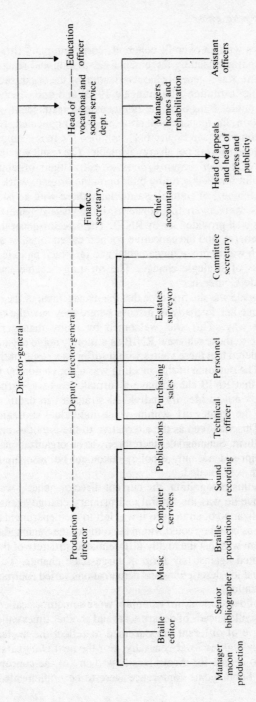

Figure 6.1 Previous structure of the RNIB (1970s) (simplified)

got to grips with an overall, coherent, corporate plan. Strategic vision was still characterized by incremental adaptation and reaction to client needs. There was a general characterization of the organization as being a 'venerable institution' (Nightingale 1973) and one which specialized in doing 'noble' things for the blind, as one respondent observed.

In addition, the management structure was fragmented. Not only was it highly complex (see Figure 6.1), but also the many support services which it required were not always available. The result was that members of executive council began to look afresh at their organization. The starting point for their scrutiny built upon the original work initiated by Boulter. Members of council, particularly those with a visual handicap themselves, were aware that concerns of the visually handicapped were not always well provided for by RNIB. The director-general, the deputy director-general, and the executive council called together a meeting in 1980 which was to prove fundamental and far-reaching in implementing the process of strategic change. The meeting became known as the Sunningdale Conference.

Sunningdale was the first time that the management of the organization had met together formally to discuss where they saw the organization going and why. This was welcomed by many managers, but was unwelcome to those who saw RNIB as a moral, noble organization and who considered that these values would suffer as a result of the proposed changes. The outcome of this meeting was a conviction by most senior managers that RNIB should have a formal, ten-year, corporate plan.

This was not to identify individual strategies in detail, but was to demarcate the framework within which individual strategies could be pursued. This was seen as the alternative to the previous era of *ad hoc* incrementalism. Sunningdale, therefore, was an organizational watershed which comprised not only a policy statement but also the recognition that change was needed.

Despite this recognition, the current director-general was in failing health. Since he was the natural and primary change agent to achieve the rationalization of strategies, it was left to the departmental managers to carry on as best they could within the remit of the Sunningdale meeting. The problem was that the highly differentiated structure of the organization mitigated against any form of large-scale change. Title, responsibilities, and job descriptions and demarcations varied enormously across the organization.

Heads of department, for example, were sometimes called directors, sometimes called heads of department, and at other times called officers. This mixture of different titles seemed to reflect the unclear thinking at the policy-making level generally. For the next two years, managers were left to decide for themselves how many of the concepts outlined during the Sunningdale conference were to be implemented in the six departments. Thus, whilst change was occurring it was doing so in an uneven and an undirected way.

The change effort was not to become orchestrated until the appointment of Ian Bruce as director-general in November 1983 following the retirement of Eddie Venn. It was clear that Bruce would pursue the process of strategic change with enthusiasm and vigour. His appointment can be seen to be the culmination of many of the themes outlined earlier, wherein the organization was perceived by many to be in need of a radical shake-up. Indeed, hard on the heels of Bruce's appointment came the pressure upon him from others in the organization to start immediately on implementing changes. Bruce, however, resisted. For one thing few policies outlined at Sunningdale were actually under way in the organization and the structure of RNIB remained unchanged, serving to stultify rather than accommodate future changes. Instead, Bruce asked for a ten-month period in which he carried out a policy feasibility study culminating in a set of poicy guidelines which were discussed through various management committees. This process also involved calling in an external consultant to look at the problems of managing strategic change. The broad terms of reference for the consultant were to: examine the organization's structure and functioning; assess the impact of future changes and to identify what adaptations might be required.

Coupled with Ian Bruce's own work as internal change agent, the consultant's report identified some major deficiencies in the structure and functioning of RNIB. These would preclude future change efforts aimed at either strategy, structure, or both. The organization was lacking clear goals. Even those strategies which could be identified readily had not been taken on board fully (or sometimes understood) by managers. Certainly, there were no clear objectives for individual departments. This lack of clarity permeated every layer of management in the organization.

Quite often, managers had drawn up their own job descriptions in the absence of any clearly specified objectives and terms of reference. Primary tasks and responsibilities of individuals were often unclear. Decision making was equally ill-defined and tediously slow. This was argued to be a result of the general lack of clarity in the structure and functioning of RNIB. For example, strategic decision making was an example of the 'constricted' type of process identified by Hickson *et al.* (1986). All decisions were concentrated on a weekly management committee meeting which had become so overloaded that insufficient attention could be given to each decision topic. Direct parallels can be seen here with the decision-making processes of Christian Aid through its strategic management team (Case Study 1: Christian Aid in this chapter).

Given the complexity of some of the issues which passed through this committee, it was also impossible to establish any priorities between topics. Even if this were the case, it was rare that decisions (and the reasons for them) were effectively communicated to the rest of the organization. Again, this is almost exactly the current picture of Christian Aid, although the delays experienced in RNIB's decision making were far more acute.

Significant areas of functional organization were missing. For example, RNIB had no marketing, public affairs or staff development functions (consultant's report: p.9). Planning, co-ordination, and integration were impossible to achieve, since future efforts in this direction relied on the existence of these functions to provide relevant information and to implement changes. Their absence also contributed to the increasing overload placed upon senior managers. In particular, certain key areas of strategic decision making were being overlooked, especially innovation and research.

The management task focused on both strategy and organizational structure. Strategy was examined first. Ian Bruce, as internal change agent, paid most attention to formulating clear policies for the organization, whilst the external consultant's review of the current deficiencies in organizational structure was used as a basis for subsequent re-structuring. This fits the view proposed by Chandler (1963) and Channon (1973) that organizational structure is a function of its strategy. Identifying strategies will almost automatically determine the kinds of structures which will support them.

Cultural change in RNIB

Simultaneously, RNIB was undergoing a major cultural change. Its prevailing culture for many years had been one of an unquestionably moral and noble organization, doing worthy deeds for a good cause. Like strategy and structure, culture in organizations is equally resistant to change and RNIB was no exception.

According to Handy (1976: 177) culture represents the 'pervasive way of life, or set of norms' in an organization. It is the accepted way of doing things. The key to unfreezing these norms in RNIB was in the recruitment of a number of managers into RNIB from outside the organizations and, in a number of cases, from outside the charitable sector altogether. The addition of these managers was of sufficient impact to break the bounds of the prevailing culture.

One RNIB manager summed up the dominantly moral culture of RNIB when he described the horrified reaction which occurred throughout the organization when he suggested taking legal action against a group of blind persons who had defaulted on payment to RNIB. This was considered to be against the spirit of the organization. In the event, no legal action ensued but the debts were repaid! This, and other similar events, began to pave the way for a culture which embraced both the compassion necessary in dealing with the visually handicapped, but which also recognized that such services can only be provided on a financially and commercially sound footing. The new managerial appointments also brought with them a break from the previously self-congratulatory culture which occasionally characterized RNIB. Coupled with complacency in the early 1970s about the continuation of government funding, this was a recipe for organizational decline. In the event, RNIB represents a charity which, although still in the throes of change processes, has successfully negotiated a complete turnaround both of strategy and structure and has averted decline.

Within just over a year there were, for the first time, a set of written and corporately agreed policy guidelines. In spring 1985, a meeting of the policy and resources committee received sixty areas of potential development for the organization which had emanated out of the consultant's report, Ian Bruce's own energetic efforts, and suggestions from newly appointed managers. In the course of discussion, this list was reduced to thirty initiatives which were to be the basis of future change.

Current strategies, structures, and change in RNIB

The new (current) structure of RNIB can be seen in Figure 6.2. Immediate differences between it and the previous structure are the standardization

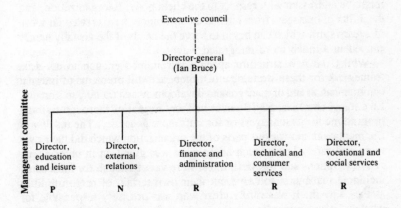

Notes:
N New post
P New person from outside organization
R Original managers with re-titled posts

Figure 6.2 Current structure of the RNIB

of departments, each of which has a director; the addition of a director of external relations where none existed before; and the abolition of the post of deputy director-general. Two new directors were appointed at this level. The post of deputy director-general was thought to be redundant in the new structure. Even in the old structure it had become a role of 'jack of all trades' where tasks not readily accomplished elsewhere in the organization were landed.

The strategies which the new structure is designed to support can be summarized as extending and rationalizing services to the blind; getting more information about the industry as a whole; pioneering new services and technology, whilst also ensuring the fullest possible integration of visually handicapped people in the community. Most of these strategic ambitions were new to the managers in RNIB.

RNIB had previously 'muddled through' (Lindblom 1959), providing a service to a set of clients who had very little choice in services provided and little say in the organization which provided them. Current strategies are more holistic. There is now an attempt to view services to the visually handicapped from a more overall point of view, with increased integration and communication between departments. One respondent described this transition as best illustrated by the rather 'cottage industry' nature of the organization some years ago, when virtually the whole organization centred around Braille and its production. Not only did this develop a kind of central elite in the organization (those who were involved in Braille) but it also precluded strategic emphasis on other issues which might be addressed with respect to the client body. Reorganization, and the influx of managers from outside the institution, have created far more of a team spirit which can begin to serve the needs of the visually handicapped in a much more integrated way.

Whilst the new structure appears streamlined enough to act as a framework for these strategic aims, there are still problems of internal communication and of management development and training to iron out. Like many charities, RNIB never had any formal or thorough training programme for its managers or for staff more generally. The result was fragmentation into various parts of the organization which did their own thing and rarely knew much about what was going on in other areas. Job descriptions and role definitions were vague enough for most staff, including managers, to carve out their own terrain of responsibilities as they saw fit. It was rarely clear who was precisely responsible for what and who could call upon the services of other parts of the organization to accomplish tasks.

To some extent, these elements persist in the current context of RNIB. Respondents were consistent in their criticism of the level of communication in the organization. Some of this is clearly the built-in inertia from the pre-Bruce era. Other problems persist, especially over the translation of corporate objectives to those members of the organization outside the limited sphere of senior management. RNIB has policies and a relatively unified cadre of managers, but it also needs to get support from the rest of the organization to implement these policies efficiently and effectively. In order to do this, it has first to overcome the inertia of its own history and then it will likely have to confront the dilemma of deciding whether it is predominantly a charitable or a professional organization (or somewhere in between).

The sea changes which the current director has proposed and which have resulted in structural reorganization, require a specificity of role and job description which has never been part of RNIB's culture. In particular, distinctions between line and staff, between demarcations of responsibility, as well as in the selection process for all staff, including senior managers, are all still rather vague and imprecise.

These are dilemmas facing a number of charities as we have seen in this book. Parallels can be drawn with the current problems of job demarcation in Christian Aid (see previous case study). RNIB has to choose between retaining a certain vagueness and ambiguity of function so that the commitment of individuals who work in the organization can be fully enjoyed, and defining roles and responsibilities more precisely so that overlaps between status, job boundaries, accountability, and seniority are reduced.

Quite apart from the above structural questions are the strategic problems and opportunities posed by the changing nature of the visually handicapped client. Not only is the client body getting older (since individuals live longer given advances in medical science and since around 60 per cent of registered blind are over 65 years old), but they are also likely to be increasingly handicapped. That is, they often suffer from multiple handicaps in addition to their visual problems. This poses a strategic question for the level and type of service provided by RNIB.

Ten years ago, children in special schools were only visually handicapped. Now, more and more students are multi-handicapped (often a combination of cerebral and visual). The Education Acts of 1970 and 1981 brought children who were defined as 'sub-normal' into the sphere of education for the first time. The transference from being previously in health care to being in the realm of education is something that RNIB was relatively slow in recognizing as an explicit demand on its services.

Other changes focus on the role of the visually handicapped in employment. Despite government policies being both complex and muddled, there are increasing opportunities in manpower resourcing than ever before. Employment schemes are opening the door for developments in this area and this is likely to be a strategic focus for RNIB now and in the future.

These changes in the environment of the visually handicapped industry have also meant the influx and emergence of other voluntary organizations which specialize in serving the visually handicapped (for example, SENS and PSSO) and which, with their higher profiles, bring increasing levels of competition for RNIB both in terms of service provision and in competing for funds from supporters. The changes have also increased

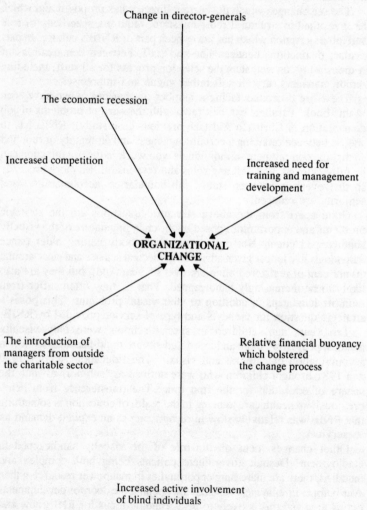

Figure 6.3 Pressures for strategic change: RNIB

the need for co-operation and joint consultation of RNIB with other organizations in the field. For example, RNIB often joins forces with other charities dealing with the blind, with Local Authorities throughout the country and uses the National Federation of Organizations for the Blind (NFB) as a voice to government. In addition, RNIB also now has a full time parliamentary officer, appointed three years ago, to increase the lobbying power of the organization toward central government. The pressures for change on RNIB are summarized in Figure 6.3.

Whilst RNIB is characteristic of an output co-operator in our analytical scheme, it is not necessarily solely in these areas that RNIB faces most difficulties. Indeed, since the stewardship of Ian Bruce, outputs have received a great deal of attention and have seen a number of modifications in order to accommodate the changing environment presented by the visually handicapped. Two areas other than outputs seem to emerge which currently, and in the future, will present strategic challenges to the organization. These are corporate image and human resource management.

Corporate image

In comparison to some of the organizations which operate in Overseas Aid, such as Oxfam or Save the Children Fund, RNIB has been remarkable in its neglect of corporate image. It is really only in the last eight years or so that serious attention has been directed toward how funders and potential funders see the organization and how the organization is viewed more generally. Public awareness of the organization has recently become a primary concern for RNIB and is likely to do so for some time to come.

It is not so much a question of whether people are aware of RNIB itself. That is without doubt. It is rather how people view the organization and how they choose to describe its culture and what it does. At one time, of course, RNIB was without doubt the only organization for the blind with which individuals would readily have identified. Now that is no longer the case. The financial implications of this in terms of sustaining inputs are obvious. Legacies have been the financial bedrock of RNIB. In the last four years, income from legacies has increased from £4 million to £10.5 million (1987). This has had the effect of bolstering internal change and facilitating expansion. For once in the voluntary sector, it is possible to say that current finance is not a major constraint!

The long-term problem with legacies is, of course, that if they are not actively sought and new ones brought on stream, they gradually tail off in number. This is just beginning to happen in RNIB and it heralds a need to emphasize the strategic management of the input side of the business rather than the outputs which has, up until now, been the long-term strategy of the organization.

It is clear across the voluntary sector that legacies predominate in what might be termed the 'established' industries of the visually handicapped, maritime, cancer, spastics, children, animals, and the National Trust (heritage). It is less clear within each industry exactly who gives by means of legacies or why they give by this means.

Given the level of fiscal competition between industries for legacies, RNIB must not only maintain its market share of legacy income, but also must increase the income raised from voluntary sources and from commercial donations. Corporate image for any voluntary organization is going to be crucial in this respect (see Wilson 1989). For one thing, commercial organizations have begun giving to specific charities (for example, the National Westminster Bank gives to Save the Children Fund). To compete, RNIB needs to move quickly and become a recognized receiver charity. Managers will have to spend a lot of time promoting organizational image. Image will also be central to effective competition, especially against newer charities which can readily catch the public eye and capture their imagination.

RNIB is some way behind many charities in image marketing. Recognition of this has prompted them to hire a fund-raising consultancy firm to bring them up to a competitive stance. Only time will tell if this is to be successful. It does, however, signal a change in strategic emphasis away from dominantly output co-operation toward input competition. If the environment of charities generally becomes more competitive, then it is likely that many organizations in the current output co-operator strategy cluster will have to concentrate rather more on inputs. RNIB is unlikely to be alone in the challenges it faces in input competition. Save the Children Fund is already likely to have shifted from this cluster into cluster two (competitive co-operators) given recent funding developments which have happened since the current data were collected. If competition continues, then it is unlikely that any charity could survive long term as an output co-operator, since changes in input sources or profiles will possibly seal the demise of the organization if they are not actively managed.

Human resource management

Like many charities, RNIB has undergone significant degrees of change in recent years and these changes have brought with them the need for resourcing at the human level as well as at the financial level. Strategic change in RNIB can be described as evolutionary (as opposed to revolutionary) but nevertheless, it is highly paced. Attempts to retain established services at the same time as introducing new services have created tensions in human resources.

First, management levels in the organization are now having to cope with far greater workloads and greater spans of control. This brings with it the need for both more professional management, possibly buying in managers from outside the voluntary sector which has occurred already to some extent, and for greater training at all managerial levels in the organization.

Second, individuals in the organization are going to have to be aware of the pace of change which is occurring in RNIB and will have to be trained to anticipate and to cope with the demands that this will place upon them both corporately and individually. For example, it is clear that certain parts of RNIB will develop rapidly and will expand, especially in fund raising and finance generally, whilst others will need to stand still and consolidate, for example, technical and consumer services or vocational and social services. It is likely that the pace of these changes will be dictated by the financial profile of the organization as the statutory agencies put greater pressure on voluntary organizations to provide services, but the success of RNIB seems to pivot upon questions of image and fund raising rather than upon any greater emphasis toward output co-operation. As one respondent said: 'Every time a guide dog walks down the street, it raises money for Guide Dogs for the Blind. Now, RNIB needs to go in for the same kind of marketing. We need to identify the needs of the visually handicapped much more precisely and ask ourselves . . . does RNIB provide a better answer to these needs than other organizations?'

Current advertising certainly takes a more aggressive stance. Adverts promote blindness as an issue, rather than RNIB as an organization. In line with this, the organization is looking toward its regional structure to try to bring fund raising regionally into line with headquarters policy. The adoption of management information systems, increased computerization, and mobile regional managers, rather than domestically fixed appointments, will help this initial impetus.

It is clear, however, that the organization bears the weight of its strategic history of incrementalism. Respondents indicated that many managers in RNIB had not really got used to thinking strategically about any kind of issue. It was difficult to think and argue toward long-term strategies. The organization has long been operating as a kind of fire brigade, often ploughing money and resources into special cases rather than into any rational or planned strategy.

One response to this, which we can also see mirrored in the Christian Aid case, is the conscious attempt to work toward priorities. This will involve a hard look at all areas of service provision (existing and planned) and rank ordering them in order of priority. The recognition that voluntary organizations can no longer be expected to work on the principle of being 'strategic sponges' – i.e. taking on all services, especially in the absence of statutory provision – appears to be a thread which permeates many of the organizations in our sample. It remains to be seen whether such a stance will be ultimately successful for RNIB and for other charities.

Case Study 3: Royal National Lifeboat Institution. An acquisitor

Introduction

RNLI emerges in this study as an organization which predominantly concentrates upon securing and extending inputs. It is this strategy which is most evident, coupled with a co-operative stance to providing services. The sub-sample of organizations with which RNLI is grouped, however, cluster primarily because of their strategic stance toward inputs rather than toward outputs. As Wilson and Butler note (1986: 529–30), RNLI really has little strategic choice over outputs since the saving of lives at sea depends upon efficiency and co-operation with other agencies such as the Royal Air Force and the Coastguard Service. RNLI is part of the cluster of organizations in which little stands out strategically apart from a high concern with efficiency of acquisition. The organization is biased *strategically toward the giver* and *operationally toward the receivers of services*. In our classification, RNLI is strategically an acquisitor. Reference to the data in Chapter 5 indicates a fairly strong *negative* weighting for extending outputs. RNLI is firmly concerned with the acquisition of inputs.

This is not to say that technical innovations and developments have not taken place within the overall context of providing a service by operating boats. The nature of boats, their design, and the different demands these place upon their crews have all undergone considerable changes especially in recent years. In addition, the way in which the overall fleet is spread around the country is subject to change over time. Nevertheless, these are changes within the overall output strategy which is itself unchanged from the genesis of the organization.

Strategy in RNLI

Initially, the organization began in rudimentary form as a self-help group with fisherman helping themselves and each other as shipwrecks occurred around the coast. Formally, RNLI was founded on 4 March 1824 following the efforts of Sir William Hillary, himself a lifeboatman. A public meeting was held in the City of London Tavern for the purpose of forming a National Institution to be supported by voluntary donations for the preservation of life following shipwreck around the coastline of England, Scotland, and Wales. In addition, the organization was to reward those who perform the rescues at sea and to grant relief to those families unfortunate enough to suffer loss of one or more of their kin as a result of the rescue attempt. This persists today in the form of a pension scheme for the widows and orphans of men who lose their lives on service.

The following extract announces the foundation of the RNLI:

> His Grace the Archbishop of Canterbury took the chair, and explained the objects of the meeting, at the same time announcing that his Majesty had been pleased to become the patron of the proposed institution. Several resolutions were then moved and agreed to, and the management of the affairs of the institution committed to the affairs of a committee of 40 gentlemen, with a Treasurer, Secretary and Assistants.

> > (*The Times*, 5 March 1824)

In fact, the royal patronage resulted in the name The Royal National Institution for the Preservation of Life from Shipwreck. This persisted until 1854, when Queen Victoria became a patron and the name of the organization became the more familiar Royal National Lifeboat Institution. Between 1824 and 1849 the Shipwreck Institution witnessed declining income. In 1849 there were ninety-six lifeboats in the Institution and over half of these were not seaworthy. Contributions had dropped from £10,000 a year to £350. There was no money to carry out essential repairs. The boats were slowly rotting.

On 4 December the 'Betsy' of Littlehampton was driven by high seas on the Hurd Sand, South Shields. A lifeboat was launched and reached the ship, only to capsize, drowning twenty of the crew and leaving seventeen widows and forty-six children to mourn. The swiftness and severity of this disaster motivated the British people to support the Institution and money began to pour into the organization. The new President, the Duke of Northumberland, offered 100 guineas as a prize for whoever designed a virtually unsinkable lifeboat. This was won by James Beeching who designed a self-righting boat, although Lionel Lucan had already proposed a similar design in the late 1700s.

The above description of income flowing into the organization hard on the heels of large disasters is one which has been constantly repeated throughout the organization's history. Between 1886 and 1891 the rising toll of lifeboats and their crews prompted the Mayor of Manchester and the Mayor of Salford to organize a parade through the streets of their towns. This raised nearly £6,000 and was the first event of its kind which was to become the now familiar Lifeboat Saturday. It also marked the first ever charity street collection in England.

More recently, the loss of the Fraserburgh lifeboat and virtually all her crew and the Penlee disaster are both well-known events which have spurred income to the organization. The obvious strategic problem is that the organization provides a constant and essential service which required equally constant financial resourcing. It is unique as a provider of this service and is supported wholly by voluntary contributions. Yet constancy in voluntary contributions is difficult to achieve and fund raising tends to decline unless it is actively managed and/or is given a shot in the arm (rather sadly) by the occurrence of another major disaster at sea.

For example, in 1968 RNLI suffered a loss in income which resulted in a deficit of around £13,000. Income had been declining over a number of years previously. Yet, when RNLI once again made headline news via two disasters (the loss of eight men at Longhope in the Orkneys, and the loss of five men in the Fraserburgh incident) the effect upon income was dramatic. The loss was rapidly converted into a surplus and, by 1970, this was running at around a quarter of a million pounds.

Public awareness of RNLI's activities is inevitably centred around disasters. Although only indicative, data from 'The Times Index' (Table 6.2) show that the occasions when RNLI appeals and activities make the newspapers are strongly correlated with the occurrence of disasters. The everyday activities of RNLI, which include the rescue of naive 'pleasure' navigators who get into difficulties rarely make headline news.

Table 6.2 Newspaper coverage of the RNLI: 1979–86: The Penlee Disaster of 1981

1979	Number of articles = 15
1980	Number of articles = 11
1981	Number of articles = 12
	Number of articles on Penlee disaster = 33
	(20–31 December)
1982	Number of articles = 9
	Penlee aftermath = 67
1983	Number of articles = 5
1984	Number of articles = 19
	Penlee Public Inquiry = 76
1985	Number of articles = 12
	(one of which was concerned with how the Penlee Trustees avoided paying tax)
1986	Number of articles = 15
	(two of which concerned Penlee)

Source: The Times Index

For example, the replacement lifeboat for the Penlee-Newlyn station made front page news stories in all the national dailies. Topics ranged from what engines the new boat was to have fitted to what she would be named. In the event, the boat was named *Mabel Alice* after the wife of Mr David Robinson of Cambridge who set up the charitable trust which donated £350,000 for the new boat. This 52-foot Arun class boat was in fact a major technological advance in lifeboat design, which RNLI had been working on over the previous ten years, although this information only made the news sporadically.

Table 6.2 shows the number of articles in *The Times* newspaper which concerned RNLI and its activities over the period 1979 to 1986. Using the categories 'Charity', 'Sea Rescue', 'RNLI', and 'Disaster', the index revealed that articles numbered, on average, twelve per year in *The Times*. On the night of Saturday 19 December 1981 the Penlee disaster occurred. The 47-foot Watson Class lifeboat *Solomon Browne* and all her crew were lost during a rescue attempt to the 1,400-ton coaster *Union Star*.

Between 20 and 31 December *The Times* ran thirty-three articles on Penlee, followed by sixty-seven articles throughout 1982 during the aftermath. Apart from the articles describing the disaster itself, there was discussion of the setting up of a public inquiry, and MPs offering advice on the distribution of the funds from the disaster appeal, and the implications of Capital Transfer Tax for the appeal. By themselves, these 100 articles are, perhaps, not surprising. Any major disaster would generate a number of articles. It is the longevity of the articles concerning Penlee which is surprising since they were still in evidence in 1986, five years after the disaster. From 1982, there were a further seventy-nine articles on the Penlee aftermath. Both the public inquiry and the potential problems with the tax laws coupled with the enormous amount of money generated by the appeal combined to keep the topic and, hence, the RNLI centre stage in the public eye.

The currency of a major disaster such as Penlee appears to be long lived. The implications of this for fund raising are crucial to RNLI. Where there is direct public awareness of RNLI through the newspapers, and other media, sustaining and extending funding levels becomes much easier. The immediacy of the impact of a major disaster is also not to be ignored. On the day following the disaster, an independent Penlee Disaster Fund was set up alongside another fund founded by local fishermen. Two quotes illustrate the point:

The response was overwhelming. Donations ranged from thousands of pounds to small amounts of silver. Many donations were anonymous, but with most came a personal letter of condolence. Gifts came from corporate bodies and associations; they came from people of all ages and all callings. Crew members from other stations collected among themselves and where they or members of branches and guilds approached the general public they were given the most wonderful support; there was no need to ask for contributions — the difficulty was in coping with the response.

So great was the response that by the time the Penwith District Council Penlee Disaster Fund was closed on February 15th, more than 2.5 million pounds had been contributed — and every penny was an expression of personal concern for those who had given so much more of so much greater value.

(*The Lifeboat* XLVIII (479): 41)

Whilst income of these proportions only follows a disaster at sea, RNLI also recognizes the boost in income which can occur following media exposure at any time. The 'Times Index' can only give a very partial indication of this effect. For example, appearances by lifeboatmen on television nearly always result in increased financial support. An appearance by an ex-coxswain of RNLI on the Michael Parkinson television show resulted in the securing of a substantial legacy in addition to a number of new and increased donations. Since legacies represent a sizeable proportion of RNLI's income (around 50 per cent), this represents a large boost to inputs. Since the Penlee disaster, a great number of television hours have been devoted to subsequent rescues and appeals for RNLI. These include, for example, *Songs of Praise*, *Blue Peter*, *Ennals Point*, the documentary series *Lifeboat*, *Jim'll Fix It*, and the recent play *Run for the Lifeboat*.

The position of RNLI within the voluntary sector is rather curious and it is possibly this *context* which accounts for the rather static picture of the organization which emerges in the course of this study. The task of the organization has remained substantially the same for over 150 years. The technology of lifeboat design and support systems has changed over the history of the organization but little else has changed in the organization of the central task or in how the organization relates to others, both voluntary and statutory.

Indeed, it is rather that changes have taken place in service provision at the level of new boats which demand new types of crews and new training to support this. Lifeboat design and support systems have changed quite markedly in the last twenty years, but the central task remains unchanged. A formal statement of the organization's mission or policy was only written down in the 1960s: 'To search and rescue up to 30 miles offshore UK and Ireland within 4 hours of launching and to remain on the scene for a further 4 hours as well as to maintain a fleet of inshore lifeboats.'

It is possibly only the increased popularity of boating as a leisure activity over recent years which has caused RNLI to embrace inshore rescue as part of its strategy and to create a club — *Shoreline* — to which people who mess about in boats can belong and through which they can donate to RNLI. Otherwise the picture is one of a relatively unchanging organization. It can afford to be. Competition for inputs and outputs is at a very low level. If individuals want to give to the cause of sea/marine rescue, they almost certainly will give funds to RNLI. There is no one else to receive such gifts.

Such strategic decisions that are made (such as the relocation of HQ at Poole rather than London) are characterized by the autonomy of the organization. Outside interests rarely interfere in decision making and any outside interests which are represented on committees are usually present only in an advisory capacity.

Furthermore, if RNLI were to stop doing its job, then the state would have to step in and either arrange for another organization to carry out the task or provide the service itself. RNLI controls a great number of contingencies in its domain. Not only is it unique, but it also does a job which would otherwise be the responsibility of the state. In addition, the cost barriers to entry for an organization considering providing a competitive service are formidable.

RNLI is an organization with a precisely defined domain of task, inputs, and services. Not surprisingly, the dominant strategy toward services (outputs) is co-operative, the key feature being co-ordinated activities between the RAF, the Coastguard Service, and the Search and Rescue Committee. The 'Government Search and Rescue Committee' is where the Department of Trade, the Ministry of Defence, and RNLI meet to discuss problems and policies. The committee also includes representatives from British Telecom and the Coastguard Service. This co-operative relationship with other statutory organizations is confined to the provision of services. It does not extend to inputs. RNLI jealously guards its financial independence from the state.

This has been the case since the 1850s when RNLI had a brief fling with state funding, but this brought with it accusations of unnecessary interference and bureaucracy with government officials at boat stations. The volume of paperwork increased considerably, was deemed inefficient, and RNLI reverted to independence, supported wholly by voluntary contributions. This stance has weathered a number of attempts to nationalize the service, most of which have been unfounded allegations of inefficiency or incompetence.

On the fund-raising side, RNLI co-operates with a host of organizations other than statutory agencies. These include, for example, commercial organizations such as Fred Olsen Lines, Mercantile Credit, Golden Wonder Crisps, and many more. Joint ventures, special concessions to 'Shoreline' members and other offers, keep the funding base of RNLI substantially in the eye of the public. Joint co-operation with other voluntary bodies is less conspicuous. Membership of the National Council for Voluntary Organizations is at best a token representation since RNLI really has very little in common with the majority of member organizations. Its very uniqueness precludes many causes of common concern across the voluntary sector. RNLI is a member of the Voluntary Movement Group, which deals with management education and training, and the International Lifeboat Federation, for which RNLI provides the permanent secretariat.

There have been brief joint activities with other charities on specific causes but these are in the minority. One of the most sustained joint activities is in lobbying government for reforms in VAT. Fuel is differentially rated, as are trailers and protective clothing. The purchase of a boat incurs no VAT liability, but launching equipment is tax payable. Other than this, however, RNLI is characterized by its lonesome, unique character.

The relative level of certainty in its domain is reflected in both the structure and the funding profile of RNLI. Very gradually, RNLI has become a decentralized bureaucracy which displays very little variation in the relative composition of its income although within overall income there is some differentiation, such as when donors make a specific request for the use of their monies. This is particularly the case with large sums when people request that a lifeboat is purchased to commemorate either themselves or one of their relatives. Twenty to twenty-five per cent of income is for the building of new lifeboats.

Taking income first, the dominant segment of income comprises legacies which have grown from 40 per cent of total annual income to around 50 per cent of total income over the last ten years. Investment income, trading profits, and membership fees have remained remarkably stable at around 4 per cent each. Voluntary donations, other than for special disasters, are again steady at around 25 per cent. Overall income is currently around £29 million.

One consequence of the relatively large amount of income through covenants and legacies is that the RNLI often does not know precisely who all the givers are. This has implications for the organization's strategy toward givers. Targeting mail, appeals, or even information is difficult. Only individuals who donate can be thus identified and kept in touch with the organization (and thanked for their donation, of course). Legacies and covenants also inevitably bring with them a certain level of anonymity.

Data on RNLI's advertising are again quite in keeping with the organization's position in its domain. As a percentage of overall income, expenditure on advertising is relatively small. It has never exceeded £450,000, which is approximately 1.5 per cent of income. This seems to reflect an organization which relies upon a fairly solid and predictable set of givers (even if they are sometimes anonymous). Such advertising strategies that are identifiable reveal a tendency to promote a slightly more aggressive message to present and future givers. Advertisements now ask us to consider 'who pays for RNLI?' rather than 'please give to RNLI, because one day your life may depend upon it'. Such changes are, however, incremental in the light of the advertising strategies of other organizations such as Oxfam, War on Want, or the Royal National Institute for the Blind.

Organizational structure

The organization structure of RNLI also appears to reflect its position of relative stability. The vast majority of its members are volunteers who man the stations around the country. Here is a fixed constituency of volunteers who almost without question and often with quite strong moral pressure from their local communities will work for RNLI. This is nowhere better demonstrated in terms of the commitment of individual boatmen and women than in the following short passage from Smiles (1898: 381). He describes the scene where a number of ships had been torn from anchor during a fierce storm. A collier-brig, one of the vessels, was adrift:

> There was not a vestige of hope for the vessel, such was the fury of the wind and the violence of the waves. There was nothing to tempt the boatmen on shore to risk their lives in saving either ship or crew, for not a farthing of salvage was to be looked for. But the daring intrepidity of the Deal boatmen was not wanting at this critical moment. No sooner had the brig grounded than Simon Pritchard, one of the many persons assembled along the beach, threw off his coat and called out, 'Who will come with me and try to save that crew?' Instantly twenty men sprang forward with, 'I will', 'And I'.

In the event, all crew were saved and landed on Walmer beach.

The voluntary nature of RNLI is immense. There are 200 lifeboat stations staffed by volunteers along with 2,000 fund-raising committees. With something like ten or fifteen volunteers per committee, there are around 35,000 fund-raising volunteers alone. This figure is, however, only an estimate and the real total may be much higher. In the UK, coxswains are paid retainers and mechanics and engineers are paid full-time by RNLI. The average lifeboat station is maintained with a minimum of ten individuals who can be called upon when needed, although larger stations can comprise up to thirty.

This 'core' of volunteers goes some way to ensure a profile of stability over time for RNLI. However, it is in the formal structure of the organization that the stability is reflected in a functionally differentiated structure. RNLI is structurally a bureaucracy. The simplified organization chart is shown in Figure 6.4.

Over its history, RNLI has become progressively more formalized

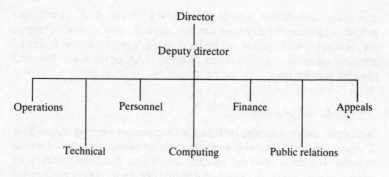

Figure 6.4 Organizational structure: RNLI

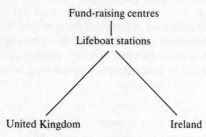

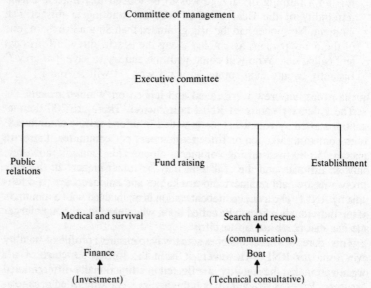

Note: Committees shown in brackets are sub-committees. They report to the main committees identified.

Figure 6.5 Committee structure: RNLI

and functionally differentiated. This accords with the findings from the larger sample, where organizations from this cluster correlate strongly with high levels of specialization and formalization. Since RNLI has a virtual monopoly over sea rescue services, it is to be expected that the organization would display all the stable and sedimented factors of a true Weberian bureaucracy.

For example, it was found necessary to set up a selection of standing committees to deal more effectively and efficiently with the various aspects of the service. Figure 6.5 shows the present committee structure. The committee of management is the policy-making forum in the organization. On it sit the president, the vice-presidents, the treasurer, and around forty other members. The Duke of Atholl is the current chairman.

The executive committee was subsequently appointed by the committee of management in order to implement policy and to manage the organization generally. Again, the Duke of Atholl is the chairman and the committee comprises fourteen other individuals including the director and the deputy director. All heads of departments report directly to the director. They are also members of a whole host of sub-committees. The committee of management will occasionally co-opt new members for their expertise, such as local knowledge, and they can in time become full members.

Along with the increase in specialization, expenditure on management support has increased substantially to cope with the extended operational scope of activities. RNLI is currently in the position of securing a stable future basis of operations by sustaining and developing this managerial base and by allocating monies to this generally.

The real question for those who support the organization as well as for the members of the organization itself remains to what extent the service offered should remain voluntary. RNLI management has in the past strongly resisted attempts to make the service statutory (either wholly or partially) and the support of vast numbers of available volunteers is another strong pressure to remain a voluntary organization. Yet the inherent stability of the task, RNLI's increasing bureaucracy and professionalization all point toward the opposite tendency. There is a case in logic for RNLI to become a statutory service. This point has already been made by a number of authors and politicians. Nightingale (1973: 86–90) makes the case forcefully for RNLI becoming statutory, arguing that since it co-operates with the Department of Trade, the Royal Air Force, and the Governmental Search and Rescue Committee, 'it would be surprising, to say the least, if co-operation were not to go further'. Eventually, 'RNLI is likely to have to accept that it cannot remain independent of the Exchequer' (p. 90).

Compelling though such arguments are, our data do not support these conclusions. The picture of RNLI presented in this book is one of an organization which has grown incrementally around a central task which has remained largely unchanged at its core. To the extent that the provision of that service requires co-operation with other statutory bodies, then this takes place, but the strategic emphasis of RNLI is not on these activities. The strategic emphasis lies in the aquisition of inputs and not in co-operating over outputs. Internal management and the services provided are largely routine matters which can be handled efficiently by the bureaucratic structure that RNLI has adopted.

It is these aspects, of course, that statutory agencies could provide equally well. Yet the combination of a strong voluntary ethos from fishing ports and seafaring people across the UK coupled with the direct labour this provides in the form of crews and support staff are irreplaceable in the statutory context. State agencies could not hope to achieve such altruistic commitment on such a large scale. The continued increase in income which RNLI has enjoyed almost every succeeding year is due in large part to this outstanding level of altruism and to the strategic efforts made by its managers and fund raisers. It is also an overall funding profile which would be extremely difficult to match given the current (and historical) fiscal policies of the state.

Case study 4: St Dunstan's. A reactor

Introduction

St Dunstan's is a charity formed in 1915 to care for ex-servicemen and women (and their families) who are registered blind as a result of their duties in HM Forces. The organization began as the brainchild of one person, Sir Arthur Pearson, when he was going blind. He was a very wealthy and influential man in London, a journalist, founder of the *Daily Express* and owner of the *Evening Standard* newspapers. He set up a care committee for soldiers and sailors which was, for the duration of the war at least, attached to the NIB (later RNIB).

The original concept for the committee was new. Each St Dunstaner would receive training at a residential centre, to equip him or her with the skills necessary for them to live an independent life, which included doing a job of work. When this training period was complete, the St Dunstaner would leave to make their own life as a civilian. It was not envisaged at the outset that any help would be given for dependants. Thus, from the start, the aim was to encourage integration of the blind into society.

St Dunstan's is included here as an example of what we have termed a 'reactor' (strategy cluster 5) organization. That is, an organization displaying such a low strategic profile as to make reference to any formal 'organizational strategy' virtually meaningless. This is certainly the case with St Dunstan's, both past and present. Due to the circumstances under which St Dunstan's came into being and the nature of its task and structure, rigid, formalized 'plans of action' have not been considered necessary (or desirable) and the history of St Dunstan's is largely one of incremental steps, evolving in response to contextual change. There have been two primary organizational aims: first, to raise enough money to complete the task set and, second, to remain as flexible as possible in order to respond quickly to changes in the environment.

The first phase

It was largely Sir Arthur Pearson's influence and leadership which gave St Dunstan's such a good start in fulfilling the first of these aims. He roused the interest of many in a position to help. Clearly, at a time of great patriotism and when emotions were easily roused, there was little difficulty in organizing events such as garden parties and placing collection boxes in most of the public houses in London to obtain the finance necessary to get the venture off the ground. It was not long after its foundation that St Dunstan's was able to obtain a suitable building for its training programme in Regent's Park. (It is in fact from this building that the organization was given its name; St Dunstan's being the name of the bell in the clock tower.) However, we cannot really talk in terms of any long-term financial strategy (or strategy of any kind) at this time since the life of St Dunstan's was envisaged to be relatively short. Pearson envisaged closure within two years after the war with the task of re-training the war-blinded complete.

It was soon apparent, however, that Pearson had misjudged the size and nature of the task in hand. First, there were many more potential beneficiaries than had been anticipated. The effects of mustard gas meant that many wounded suffered a gradual loss of sight and this had not been predicted. There were also those who were more severely injured and had lost limbs as well as their sight, and the problems these people faced were more complex, needing more special attention. Second, it was realized that the original intention of simply training men for independence was inadequate. A comprehensive aftercare service was needed. To meet this need, a team of welfare visitors was recruited to work nation-wide, making regular and emergency visits in order to help iron out any problems the St Dunstaner might have. Allied to this was an Estates Department which bought and rented homes to St Dunstaners, perhaps enabling them to move to a job. This department also arranged mortgages for those able to buy houses. Third, it was realized that the provisions must also include dependants and a separate children's fund was set up. The system works in virtually the same way today.

On the whole, the first few years after the war witnessed a great expansion in the remit of the organization as the full effects of the war became apparent and it was realized that in order to fulfil its task the organization needed to do much more than simply re-train ex-servicemen. This expansion also made the tasks facing St Dunstan's much clearer which it could best achieve as an independent organization and thus, at the end of the war, it detached itself from the NIB and became a separate entity.

The second phase

However, Sir Arthur Pearson died suddenly, in 1921. His death was a great shock to all those involved with St Dunstan's. Pearson had been the driving force behind the organization and his character was firmly stamped upon the place.

His obvious successor was a young man 24 years old, who had been blinded during the war and had been working for St Dunstan's as a welfare officer. Ian Fraser (later Lord Fraser) had been Pearson's right-hand man, and had also married Pearson's secretary, Irene Mace. Lady Pearson had also become president after her husband's death, a post she held well into the 1940s. Fraser had the same kind of pioneering spirit as his predecessor, and he became something of a champion for the blind, pressing for better state pensions and recognition of the needs of blind people.

At this time (1923) St Dunstan's was a registered company with approximately 2,000 beneficiaries; ran nine or ten holiday homes, a training centre in London; had a nation-wide system of welfare provision, administered pensions to all St Dunstaners and ran estates and appeals departments.

Despite the flying start that St Dunstan's had received under the leadership of Pearson, the slump of the 1920s and 1930s hit the organization very hard. In fact, it only just survived. All ten holiday homes were closed in the retrenchment which was necessary. The measures taken by Ian Fraser were indeed drastic. It is said that he arrived at the office one Monday morning and the first thing he did was to cut salaries by half and also halve the number of staff! The appeals department was put into overdrive. Fortunately, the organization had begun to receive generous legacies by this time and this, coupled with a revitalized appeals effort, the reduced labour costs, and profits from the sale of property meant St Dunstan's pulled through.

With the rigours of the slump behind them, St Dunstan's could plan, once again, to the future. In 1938 Ian Fraser House was built in Brighton for use as a holiday home, but with the advent of the Second World War this was needed as a second training centre. An ophthalmic operating theatre was added to the building in 1939.

The Second World War heralded the second phase of development for St Dunstan's. The developments were five-fold; first, the war effort meant that many more blind people would be placed in employment after training. The 1930s had witnessed a significant fall in the numbers of St Dunstaners who found work on completion of training. During the Second World War, the situation improved tremendously. Second, a new generation of war blinded needed to be catered for. But these were a different type of casualty: for example, there were no gas casualties and immediate numbers did not rise as fast as in the First World War. There were more casualties from the Far East war camps, and many more with a gradual loss of vision. Third, the beneficiaries from the First World War were now reaching middle and old age and steps would need to be taken to accommodate the change in emphasis needed, for example, away from training for work toward training for leisure. Fourth, with more people being placed in employment the demand for housing increased and, therefore, the activities of the housing department were stepped up. Finally, it was decided at this stage that careful monitoring of the financial situation was needed in order for St Dunstan's to meet its obligations to beneficiaries. It should still be remembered that the eventual closure of St Dunstan's is always on the agenda, and from the time of the Second World War, regular financial reports from actuaries were, and are, received with forecasts concerning the fund-raising effort required to obtain sufficient finance to fulfil the task set.

The third phase

The third and final phase in St Dunstan's history, that of a gradual reduction in size, coupled with a continuing change of emphasis in services, began in 1960 with the decision to reduce all forms of competitive fund raising. For example, the 'darts boxes' in public houses were withdrawn and given to RNIB. In 1966 *all* appeals were stopped, the rationale being that the organization had sufficient reserves to be able to rely upon legacy income and spontaneous donations. The appeals and publicity department became the public relations department as a result of these decisions, and considerable effort was made to explain to regular donors why the decisions had been made. These decisions did, in fact, indicate the recognition that, although the organization was still very busy, a 'wind-down' had really begun in earnest. As staff retired, they were not replaced and for the past twenty years or so there has been a gradual streamlining of the organization. The public relations department, for example, in 1960 had twenty-two staff. At present it totals eight. Many of the first generation St Dunstaners have now passed away, and numbers are gradually falling. There are still new beneficiaries, from the Falklands war and Northern Ireland, but, at present, the date for the termination of the organization is set for early next century.

However, the final phase is not one characterized by stagnation. This has been a time of change. In 1961, the institution was amended to provide for the payment of allowances to wives, widows, children, and anyone who has contributed significantly to the care of a St Dunstaner. The welfare department, although dealing with fewer numbers, finds itself coping with the inevitable problems that old age coupled with blindness and multiple handicaps bring.

This final phase has also witnessed more upheaval than the other two due to changes in leadership. Lord Fraser dominated phases 1 and 2 and a large part of phase 3. In 1974 he died, aged 77 years. He was succeeded by Ian Garnett-Orme, who, it is generally felt, had a more sensitive approach to the task than his predecessor, who could perhaps be accused of being somewhat 'old fashioned' in some of his views. Garnett-Orme began to make the changes necessary to meet the needs of wives and widows more fully. He retired in 1983 and was replaced by Sir Henry Leech, who has continued with this emphasis. An example of the change in attitude is the refurbishment of Ian Fraser House to include accommodation for married couples and also the introduction of a licensed bar only four years ago.

The strategic history of St Dunstan's is largely one of response to a felt need and to contextual change; the gradual inclusion of dependants as beneficiaries and the change in emphasis away from training toward leisure are examples of this. There appear to be four main reasons why this type of management has been prominent.

First, at the outset it was not envisaged that St Dunstan's would be in existence for any great length of time. Pearson's intention was to re-train the war-blinded, not to provide any kind of social services; once all the war-blinded were re-trained, then St Dunstan's would no longer be needed. As has already been noted, he underestimated the task involved, perhaps because of an oversimplified vision of the kinds of problems the war-blinded would face and hence the type of help that would be needed. It is almost certain also that he underestimated the numbers of casualties that there would be.

Second, it was clearly impossible to plan for the Second World War and its effects. Thus, no plans would have been made to prolong the life of St Dunstan's beyond that which was needed for the first generation of St Dunstaners. Indeed, any long-term strategy that had been made would need to have been either scrapped or radically altered in the light of the far-reaching effects of the Second World War.

Third, and more important, is the environment in which St Dunstan's operates. The task environment is relatively simple and stable. In comparison to RNIB, with its size and diversity, St Dunstan's is a very simple organization. First of all, it deals with a very specific group of people — the war-blinded and their families. It does not deal with blind children, for example. Many St Dunstaners are now either retired or coming up to retirement age. Therefore, St Dunstan's deals with a fairly homogeneous group in terms of disability and age range. As the number of St Dunstaners falls, the task of caring for surviving St Dunstaners becomes easier — with fewer people to care for, more resources become available. Dealing with a small clientele also enables the organization to adopt a fairly flexible stance with regard to services provided. For example, a St Dunstaner may wish to move home in order to take up a new job, but cannot find suitable accommodation. St Dunstan's has been known to build purpose-built homes, suited to a St Dunstaner's particular needs.

The external environment is fairly stable. Unless there is a war in the near future, there is very little that will radically alter St Dunstan's' task or the way it is carried out. Indeed, the relative simplicity of the task has meant no radical changes have taken place since the organization began, and this has rather precluded the need for detailed strategic plans.

In addition, the organization has always been dominated by the personality of the chairman. There have been only four in the entire history of St Dunstan's and one of these, Lord Fraser, held the position for fifty-three years! This has meant a highly centralized system of decision making, the finance and general purposes committee (see Figure 6.6) making most policy decisions and the executive committee simply

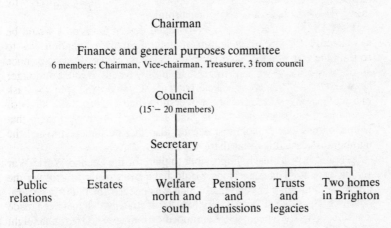

Note : Both finance and general purposes committee meet quarterly. Normally arranged for same day.

Figure 6.6 Organizational structure: St Dunstan's

informing heads of departments of the decisions made. This is not to say that heads of departments (or anyone else) do not have direct access to those above them; everyone is at liberty to approach anyone with suggestions or grievances. But it has meant that the ethos of the organization and the types of services it provides are largely dependent on the personality, charisma, and attitude of the chairman. To a certain extent also the flexibility of the organization and its ability to respond to changes has also been dependent on the ability of the chairman and the members of the executive committee to foresee particular problems or trends and to respond in the appropriate way.

The final question then remains: what will happen to St Dunstan's if there is not another war? As yet the answer appears to be that the organization will cease to function early in the next century. There is talk of some kind of merger with other ex-servicemen organizations with which St Dunstan's has close links. Perhaps another task will be found. As yet there are no definite plans.

Chapter seven

Analysis of the case studies

As pointed out in Chapter 6, the intention was to have one detailed case study from each of the five clusters of strategy identified in the data analysis. In the event, we were able to secure access to four organizations. These were RNLI, RNIB, St Dunstan's, and Christian Aid. Each of these four organizations is in a different strategic cluster, although this leaves cluster one (Extenders) without a representative detailed case. However, the authors of this book have had significant contact with Oxfam over a number of years looking at such factors as its strategy and structure, its perceived image, and the organization's marketing strategies. Since Oxfam is a cluster one (Extender) organization, these data will be drawn upon in place of a formal case study and the data will be presented as the chapter unfolds.

The aim of this chapter is to illustrate in some detail the complex interaction of these organizations with their changing environments and their specific strategic responses. The ways in which the case study organizations cope with such change processes should also shed further light on the characteristics of each of the five strategic clusters identified in Chapter 5. The organizations chosen for detailed analysis are shown in Table 7.1. The keynote theme of all these detailed cases lies in the challenge of strategic and structural change. All these organizations face changing environments, yet their responses to such demands have been diverse and variously successful. Initially, it is useful to distinguish between active and passive response to changes.

Table 7.1 The case study organizations

Organization	Strategy type	Context
Oxfam	Extender (EX)	Dynamic 1
Christian Aid	Competitive co-operator (CC)	Service
RNIB	Output co-operator (OC)	Dynamic 2
RNLI	Acquisitor (AQ)	Niche
St Dunstan's	Reactor (RE)	Protected

Active strategic responses to change

The first three organizations in the above table (Oxfam, Christian Aid, and Royal National Institute for the Blind) have all responded actively. That is, they have all engaged in often quite radical strategic and structural changes in response to, and in anticipation of, environmental or sectoral demands. As an Extender, Oxfam has much in common with the strategies pursued by other organizations in its cluster. War on Want, for example, has begun to adopt an extremely flexible approach to service provision at the same time as trying to reduce a rather overly 'political' image. This kind of proactive strategic behaviour is typical also of the British Red Cross, Jewish Blind Society, and Voluntary Services Overseas (see Chapter 5). The hallmark of these kinds of organizations is their capacity or their ability to achieve change through constant self analysis prior to the occurrence of any external events which may eventually force the strategic change process.

RNIB and CAID also have embarked upon proactive strategies although they occupy different strategic clusters outlined in Chapter 5. Their proactivity lies in both professionalization of management and structural changes in the organization. CAID has undergone a greater degree of structural change than any other organization from our sample. Both professionalization and structural change are increasingly common hallmarks of recent activity in the voluntary sector (see Wilson 1989). This is also true of many of the other organizations from cluster two (competitive co-operators) and cluster three (output co-operators).

Royal Commonwealth Society for the Blind (cluster two, competitive co-operators), for example, is rapidly embarking upon a programme of professionalization with the aim of changing organizational image from old colonial to modern and flexible. Structural changes have also occurred and are best reflected in the differential strategies that are now being adopted toward its different countries of operation.

Passive responses to change

The remaining two case study organizations have shown evidence of some changes, but these are relatively passive in relation to their operating environment. Both RNLI and St Dunstan's have grown incrementally around a central and almost unchanging task (Lindblom 1959). St Dunstan's (STDS) strategic history is one of almost total passivity. Its central strategy of helping the war blinded expanded to include running homes, providing training and rehabilitation, and then ceased to change at all. Passivity in STDS is particularly marked by the orientation of its managers who view the organization as being at the end of its life cycle with the demise of the organization likely to occur in the next few years.

In the case of RNLI, the dominant strategies have been largely passive responses to changes in its operating environment. Saving life at sea has remained the dominant task and the organization's unique position as the only provider of these services has contributed to shaping its strategic profile. Changes have occurred largely in technology and in organizational structure, both of which have been aimed at maintaining efficiency in the provision of existing services. For example, the increased popularity of sail-boarding and pleasure boating has meant an increased number of casualties who get themselves into difficulties very quickly. This has meant that the speed of lifeboats has had to keep pace and advanced technology in lifeboat design has facilitated this. Nevertheless, from a strategic perspective, the central task of saving life at sea by means of lifeboats remains the same.

Changes in strategy and structure

Oxfam, Christian Aid (CAID), and Royal National Institute for the Blind (RNIB) have all undergone varying degrees of metamorphosis to their central tasks and, as we have seen, have approached their environments proactively. It is noticeable in these organizations that a consistent pattern of structural change occurs alongside strategic readjustments, and that this is always toward decentralization. In Christian Aid's case, the structural change toward decentralization was abrupt. The organization adopted a matrix structure effectively 'overnight', a radical departure from its previous structure, a centralized bureaucracy. Oxfam and RNIB have chosen to decentralize in a less radical form, although at the time of writing Oxfam are considering the matrix form as one alternative for the future and for further decentralization to be desirable.

The arguments in favour of decentralization and for matrix forms of organizational structure are particularly seductive in the voluntary sector. This is hardly surprising given that decentralization has been a common message in virtually all sectors, public and private as well as the voluntary sector. In the name of significantly increased performance and organizational effectiveness, Peters and Waterman (1982) and Kanter (1984) have been among the most evangelical of the advocates of decentralization. Their work concerns solely commercial organizations, yet the words of the authors of the 'New Testament' (if *In Search of Excellence* was the 'Old Testament') indicate very much how the concept is rooted in the values of altruism and voluntarism. Peters and Austin (1985: 210) state: 'But you cannot order anyone to perform in an excellent fashion — "excellent" meaning courteous, creative. Excellence, by its very definition and at all levels, is a purely voluntary commitment. It ensues only if the job is sincerely "owned".' (Authors' original emphasis.)

Translate these statements into the world of charities, overlay them with moral commitment and the ideology of altruism and you brew a potent recipe indeed! Whilst the idea of commitment both to organizational and to personal beliefs and ideals may be slightly strange to many individuals in the commercial world, it is highly synonymous with the values and beliefs of many who work for charities. Thus, the adoption of structures such as matrices can seem 'natural'. They appear to fit both personal and organizational values.

Analysis of the cases does reveal that all is not plain sailing despite the seemingly natural fit between the values of individuals and organizational structure. We explore the reasons for this in the next sections.

The trend towards decentralization

The histories of Oxfam, CAID and RNIB are curiously similar in one respect. All began as extremely flexible, small organizations under the strong leadership of one or two visionary 'founding fathers'. As each organization persisted, operational complexity demanded at the least a formal structure coupled with a growth in organizational size. Already, the beginnings of an organizational life cycle are apparent (Kimberly and Miles 1980) with a transition from small, entrepreneurial organization, all under the control and guidance of one individual, to a more mature phase where the organization grows and develops beyond the control of a single individual.

As support systems grow in complexity and size, the need for hierarchy, professional management, and organizational control mechanisms becomes apparent. Both CAID's and RNIB's response to this were somewhat different to that of Oxfam. It is worth spending some time describing events in Oxfam since not only do they differ markedly from the responses of the other organizations, but also Oxfam seems to have avoided, for the time being at least, some of the dysfunctions of adopting either a purely centralized or a totally decentralized structure. CAID and RNIB have been characterized by massive changes in structure and strategy. Oxfam appears to have had a steadier change process throughout its history.

Although Oxfam responded to an increase in size by proliferating committees in its organization, the demarcation between operating and policy sectors was deliberately maintained. So, too, were relatively generous levels of fiscal and strategic autonomy to those operating overseas in the field. The result of this is very similar to Chandler's (1963) divisionalized structure, although all the divisions are in headquarters in the case of Oxfam (except the overseas field staff, of course). A brief sketch of the current structure of Oxfam is shown in Table 7.2.

Table 7.2 Organizational structure: Oxfam, 1987

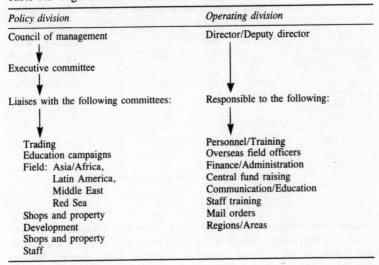

Policy division	Operating division
Council of management	Director/Deputy director
↓	
Executive committee	
↓	↓
Liaises with the following committees:	Responsible to the following:
↓	↓
Trading	Personnel/Training
Education campaigns	Overseas field officers
Field: Asia/Africa,	Finance/Administration
Latin America,	Central fund raising
Middle East	Communication/Education
Red Sea	Staff training
Shops and property	Mail orders
Development	Regions/Areas
Shops and property	
Staff	

Oxfam is characterized by decentralization particularly during the 1970s, yet this was achieved in conjunction with preserving overall strategic control of the organization both at the director and the executive committee level. In many respects, this corresponds to the combination of 'loose and tight coupling' advocated by Peters and Waterman (1982). For Oxfam, this appears to have been successful. Income levels have shown a consistent growth each year. Oxfam has also been a consistent market leader since 1981. It has been in the top four charities (measured by income) with a turnover of approximately £42 million in 1987 (year end 1 April), £45 million in 1986 and £50 million in 1985. The organization also does fairly well on a number of other criteria according to data from other recent research (see Swords 1987: 34). A sample of 353 respondents in the UK indicated that public perception of Oxfam was one of a traditional/respectable charity. Its profile is much like that of the British Red Cross which also falls into the extender strategic cluster. These data of public perceptions of the charities reported in Swords (1987) are summarized in Table 7.3.

The decentralization patterns of both CAID and RNIB appear rather less obviously planned processes. They represent radical responses to pressures on the organization from both within and from the immediate external environment. In both cases, these organizations were effectively shaken by the scruffs of their necks and catapulted into new strategic directions alongside the adoption of their new structures. In RNIB the

Analysis of the case studies

Table 7.3 Nine perceptual dimensions of six charities
Percent of sample population responses (n = 353 respondents)

	Oxfam	Action Aid	Christian Aid	Red Cross	Save the Children	War on Want
Being established	62	3	33	87	36	12
Not political	48	23	39	48	40	22
Relief work	62	13	29	70	29	15
Long-term projects	39	15	30	26	17	13
Responsive	27	17	14	33	25	10
Uses donations well	43	21	31	51	41	13
Administration costs controlled	33	18	24	35	28	18
Large organization	72	9	31	83	46	11
Often makes appeals	47	13	29	30	61	15

Source: Swords (1987: 34)

vision came from one man, Ian Bruce, who was appointed director-general in November 1983. In CAID, the pressure for change came from the report of an external consultant coupled with growing feelings amongst staff of unrest and dissatisfaction.

It is worth noting at this stage the similarities in the history of strategic management in both CAID and RNIB. Prior to change occurring, both organizations had reached a point of no return. They were faltering both in sustaining support from their constituency of givers as well as from their employees. In the language of organizational change processes, the resultant change strategies were 'crisis driven' (Pettigrew 1985). Prior to the changes, management style in both organizations was non-directive and essentially *laissez-faire*. There was no clear corporate strategy nor any clear guidelines for where the organization was going even in the short term. RNIB had become institutionalized, whilst CAID had grown piecemeal to be dominated by one functional department (Aid). Organizational survival during this period was secured less by overt management skills, but more through the body of committed employees who sustained the organization with their energy and enthusiasm which went far beyond any formal job description.

When these organizations decentralized, they did it in a radical way. This is to be predicted if we follow the literature on organizational change at this level of analysis. There was internal unrest in the organization, coupled with ruminations on a desired future state of affairs married to the context of retiring or resigning senior management and the appointment of an outsider as director. These are argued to be almost 'classic' features of major change processes (see, for example, Leontiades 1980, Pettigrew 1985). Politically and culturally, the stage is set for a major transformation to take place. Support for the change is mobilized from within the organization and the appointment of an outsider legitimizes the 'new broom' effect.

It would be only a partial analysis, however, if we were to concentrate upon the question of decentralization without reference to the context of each organization. Whilst RNIB and CAID have changed structurally and strategically, both organizations still operate within a largely unchanged context. CAID still operates within the aegis of the British Council of Churches, is still not active operationally overseas, and still has to gain support from largely an ecumenical constituency. This begs the question not of whether the change process was necessary or not, but rather asks the managers of all charities if the form or structure of organization, currently in operation, is appropriate to the context in which it operates?

Decentralization and change in context

One strong theme which underlies the cases, and many of the organizations described in Chapter 5, is the tension between the need for formal organization and support systems on the one hand and the needs of staff to preserve both autonomy and personal development on the other. Couple this with strong, personalized leadership and the potential for conflict within the organization is heightened. In all the cases except RNLI, the role of leaders, visionaries, and recent change agents at the helm of the organization is notable.

Just to take this aspect of voluntary organizations would tempt their classification as 'power cultures' (Handy 1976), where the organization can be characterized structurally as a spider's web with the all-powerful spider at the centre who controls all organizational processes. Looking further than this, the organizations in the case studies are also all partially 'person cultures'. That is, each individual in the organization seeks actively not to be constrained by formal job descriptions, but tries to preserve the facility to expand their skills and expertise into a number of different areas. Respondents in all the case study organizations, and in many of the organizations in the wider sample were at pains to point out the need to have the potential for personal and professional development in their jobs and bemoaned their lot where they felt hemmed in by overly restrictive job descriptions.

Further analysis also reveals perceived needs by both senior and middle level staff for the organization to have systems of control, of role and of regulation of job activities since this is felt to be one way of ensuring that staff are not needlessly replicating or straying into one another's jobs. On these criteria, elements of Handy's 'role culture' could be attributed to the case organizations. Co-ordination by management teams, the formation of standing committees, the need for effective and formalized communication patterns are all aspects of the role culture. This kind of formal, role-defined organization is also evident from the organizations in the wider sample. Apart from the three organizations in cluster 5 (the reactors; see Chapter 5), managers in virtually all the sample organizations were concerned with achieving greater precision in the demarcation of functions, who performed identified tasks, where and when.

A profound tension is therefore going to exist in these organizations. Diverse, and arguably irreconcilable, cultures appear to vie with one another for primacy. People need to be individualistic. But this is difficult to achieve in an organization which also needs some forms of control to monitor performance and to demarcate tasks. In an organization which is small and expanding it is possible for such task ambiguity and control mechanisms to coexist. Personalized leadership can keep a check on organizational performance and other individuals can carve out their own space in the expanding organization.

Once the organization grows beyond the control and oversight of one individual, the need for formal control mechanisms inevitably occurs. Furthermore, the room for individuals essentially to define their own jobs and their own personal work space decreases. The two factors of increasing organizational size and organizational maturity, as systems of administration and control develop, mitigate against individualism (Kimberly and Miles 1980). However, even formal procedures and task definitions are not enough to steer the organization toward future strategic goals. Thus, strong and visionary leaders are also required who are committed to the central tasks or *raison d'être* of the organization. The clash between all these cultures (power, task, and role) manifests itself in different ways in voluntary organizations and each carries with it some lessons for their management.

In St Dunstan's (STDS), for instance, the clash of cultures never arose. This charity never made it to the stage of formal organization. STDS remained effectively solely a power culture driven by its charismatic and influential leaders. Its founder, Sir Arthur Pearson, envisaged closing the whole operation only two years after its foundation, since he believed that the demand for STDS's services would only last this period. He was to be proven wrong, but the effect of his belief was that STDS was a 'one-man show'. Even his successor, Ian Fraser, maintained the same philosophy of management as his predecessor. The organisation was solely a power culture.

This was particularly so in the 1920s and 1930s when STDS faced fiscal crises along with many other organizations in the visual handicapped sector. Fraser steered the organization through this without any formal organizational support at all. STDS recovered, but it has gradually reduced in size since the 1960s. There were no pressures to formalize, or to decentralize, for that matter. The organization neither became large nor complex enough for these issues to be faced. A strong leader was enough to steer the organization along. RNLI, on the other hand, achieved the status of a complex and formal organization relatively quickly. Like STDS, the clash of cultures outlined above never arose in this organization either. RNLI is characterized by an overwhelming unity of strategic purpose which was stamped upon the organization at birth. Just as St Dunstan's was only concerned with the war-blinded (and no other group of visually handicapped people), RNLI's task of sea rescue (and no other form of rescue) was equally well defined. Apart from technological changes along the way in lifeboat design, for example, there has been little change in RNLI's central task. A relatively complex organizational structure has grown around this task. The aim of the structure is primarily concerned with securing efficiency in gaining inputs (money and people) into the organization. In Weberian terms, it is close to an ideal-type bureaucracy (Weber 1947). Current strategic concerns focus upon the nature of the service provided by lifeboats. Since lifeboats are now faster than ever before, it is likely that future strategic directions will include a much improved lifeboat service overall, rather than a reduced number of stations to provide the same level of service.

This is also in line with a broad systems' view of organization (Burns and Stalker 1961, Lawrence and Lorsch 1969). RNLI's environment is relatively static and predictable. It is almost unique as a provider of sea rescue services by means of lifeboats. The rate of change in this operating environment is also relatively incremental and, to some extent predictable, so there is little need for the organization to be strategically flexible in the traditional way argued to characterize voluntary organizations outlined in Chapter 2 of this book. RNLI is something of an exception to this 'rule'.

Thus a decentralized bureaucratic structure is ideally suited to RNLI's environment (Burns and Stalker 1961, Lawrence and Lorsch 1969). Even though the operating environment is changing faster than ever before, largely due to an increase in the popularity of water sports and water-based hobbies, which in turn demand advances in lifeboat technology, the strategy and structure of RNLI are congruent to its wider domain.

Thus far, we have discussed aspects of charitable organization such as structure, strategy, and cultures in isolation. This is necessary as an analytical device, but it does not reflect the reality of the management task. Managers of charities face the complex task of handling all these aspects simultaneously. This presents them with a level of complexity even greater than we have revealed so far. We discuss some of the problems which can arise out of managing this complexity in the next section.

Managing strategy, culture, and structure

The analysis outlined above raises some fundamental questions for the management of charities both today and in the future. Unless the environment is extremely benign and the charity virtually unique (as in the case of RNLI), the operating context of charitable organizations requires active and future oriented management. This will involve attention to strategy as well as to organizational culture and structure.

The data presented in this book point to the increasing rate and pace of changes which impact upon most charitable organizations. In addition, many of these organizations have reached the stage in their life cycle where neither visionary leaders alone, nor *laissez-faire* systems will suffice. Whilst all charitable organizations must satisfy to some degree the motivational commitment of their staff, they cannot afford to neglect the dysfunctional aspects of organization that ineffective, or inappropriate, management can bring about. We examine below some of these problems which come out of the data from both the cases and the wider sample.

Communication problems

Exemplified by CAID and, to a lesser extent by Oxfam, the problem of maintaining effective communication internally between functions and maintaining effective communication externally, including creating and maintaining organizational image and securing givers, is often sizeable.

In the case of CAID, the implementation of a matrix structure may have seemed a logical alternative toward satisfying staff participation in decision making, but it also brought with it severe communication problems. For example, the implementation of a strategic management team (SMT) meant that whilst all departments had access to the decision-making forum, the sheer volume of issues to be decided upon by this body created a severe communication problem. It was rarely clear to anyone other than SMT members precisely what was on the agenda, or what had been decided (if anything) since agendas were prepared hastily in advance of meetings and minutes were often unintelligible to the extent that linking actions taken/recommended with agenda items was impossible. Even amongst members of SMT itself, it was often said that it was unclear in some cases whether a decision had been taken or not.

Unlike Oxfam, where operating, strategic, and policy decisions were clearly demarcated to be dealt with in specific parts of the organizational structure, CAID tended to push all decisions toward SMT. This merely added to the volume of issues to be handled as well as added to the communication problems between SMT and the rest of the organization. This is not to say that Oxfam is without communication problems, despite attempts to classify decision arenas into strategic and operational. As

Swords (1987) and Masson (1986) argue, the major problem facing Oxfam is one of securing effective communication internally between divisions and departments. One side of the organization can be unaware what another side is doing.

For example, the launch of a major new lobbying campaign, 'Hungry For Change' (1984), was an Oxfam venture designed to involve supporters in the underlying causes of poverty and to raise the level of public awareness concerning the problems facing developing countries. The campaign includes lobbying members of Parliament and central government agencies to take more positive actions in their relationships with developing countries. The concern of Oxfam's fundraising division is that pursuit of such a strategy will have possibly deleterious effects upon the more 'traditional' supporters of Oxfam, both in terms of financial input and the number of available volunteers. The campaign was launched, however, without clear prior communication between departments. Although decentralized, Oxfam appears to have a problem of ineffective lateral communication across functional areas.

This is because Oxfam is operating as a set of autonomous divisions. This is fine for securing planning autonomy in each individual operational sector. It is also beset with problems if effective co-ordination of each of these actions is not achieved. The management task in Oxfam would seem to be primarily one of increasing the efficacy of co-ordination rather than improving leadership or strategic trajectories.

Preserving local autonomy

A further set of management problems evident from the cases is that of the pressure amongst departments and divisions to preserve and further their professional and strategic autonomy. Put simply, this is an extension of the idea of 'local rationality' proposed by Cyert and March (1963) with respect to decision making. These authors argued that rational decision making became unrealizable in most firms because structure mitigated against it.

Dividing an organization up into departments meant that each department saw issues from its own local, or self-interested, perspective and acted accordingly. Local autonomy is a similar idea prompted by the case study data. It means that there is a strong tendency for divisions and departments to retreat into their respective shells, go it alone and devise their own strategies to local problems rather than acknowledge or face any overall corporate structural problem or deficiency.

The proliferation of working groups, special *ad hoc* committees and other alternative decision or operating fora are examples of the symptoms of local autonomy. Both CAID and Oxfam give evidence of this occurring. One explanation might be the extraordinary commitment to, and identification with, organization values that is evidenced in staff. This concurs with Rokeach's (1968: 4–21) notion of 'existential and non-existential' belief structures. As he notes: 'The more a given belief is functionally connected or in communication with other beliefs, the more implications and consequences it has for other beliefs and, therefore, the more central the belief'. (p. 5)

The central beliefs held by the staff of charitable organizations are not only congruent with organizational cultures and prevailing ideologies in a way almost never found (but often strived for) in commercial organizations, but they also seem strong enough for organizational goals to be subsumed by personal aims. That is, individuals and departments will take on more and more or, alternatively, go it alone rather than attend first to any corporate organizational ills. The way forward is seemingly to attend to and develop personal ambitions and values and thus increase autonomy at this local level.

The decision of the education sector in CAID not to participate in the matrix structure is one example of this effect taking place. So is the stance taken by UK/Ireland overseas group which, although structurally included in the matrix structure, largely operates outside it. Other examples of departments 'doing their own thing' as a first choice can be found in virtually all the cases. It can also be found at the organizational level of analysis. In particular, the relationship between headquarter organization and area staff in both CAID and Oxfam exemplify local autonomy operating between different parts of the organization in relation to headquarters. Complaints from area staff in both organizations concerning their relationship and communication with headquarters centred around this issue. Respondents said that communication really depended upon who you know in headquarters rather than what you knew about organizational functioning. Area staff in both Oxfam and CAID felt that headquarters were impregnable and their strategic actions difficult to predict. Communication was one way, from headquarters to area, and managers in headquarters had a tendency to take actions without informing area staff until after it had taken place.

A question of over-decentralization?

Linked with the above issues is the question of decentralization. Virtually all the case study organizations, with the exception of RNLI, were characterized by on-going processes of decentralization. The case study of RNIB provides a good example of issues which arise as a result of decentralization and which were possibly not anticipated in the overall drive toward relaxing hierarchical control and increasing participation. These issues are likely to hold true for a great number of other charities and they represent fundamental problems in the current and future management of charities.

Three major points emerge:

1. Decentralization means that decisions take longer as more and more people are involved in the process. This occurs irrespective of whether the decision topic is considered to be strategic, operational, or relatively trivial. It also means that managerial levels necessarily experience a substantial increase in their span of control. This can be seen to be an important issue in RNIB, CAID and Oxfam. It may also have implications for the type of manager recruited in the future. Selection of managers is likely to include the ability to handle large spans of control and to operate effectively in decision-making fora. In particular, it implies a trend toward recruiting professional management which is sourced from outside the charitable sector.

In turn, this means that such managers may not possess the same degree of commitment, altruism, and selflessness which characterized some of their predecessors who were 'traditionally' always in the charitable sector. The knock-on effect of recruiting a substantial number of professional managers is likely to involve further changes to corporate strategy, to staffing levels, and possibly to corporate image as the lessons learned by managers in the commercial sector are translated wholesale into the charitable sector (see Wilson 1989).

2. Almost paradoxically, the process of decentralization brings with it the need for precise job and role specificity at all levels in the organization. Demarcations of responsibility have to be made clear in order to avoid needless replication of tasks and to ascertain who has responsibility for them. RNIB is currently wrestling with this problem since the culture of the organization built up and sedimented over many years is one which resists such precision of specification. CAID faces the same set of problems. Matrix organizational structures, such as Christian Aid, are extreme forms of decentralization, yet it is often overlooked that it requires a commensurately high level of precision in role and task definition before such structures can work effectively. Otherwise, those individuals who are at the centre of all matrix 'projects' (in CAID's case, this means all the members of SMT) are the only ones whose task is sufficiently well demarcated, and they get all the decision-making jobs in the organization leaving the rest of the staff to carry on as before.

3. Possibly most important of all is that decentralization highlights the distinction between the management process and task accomplishment. It separates out the 'managers' from the 'doers' in any organization (see Knight 1974, Child 1984, Galbraith 1973). It also begs the question of whether those who manage can be the same individuals as those who carry

out the tasks of the organization directly, or whether there should be some sort of separation. The most acute form of this dilemma can be seen in the CAID case, although Oxfam appears to be suffering to a lesser extent from the same problems.

The management and design of voluntary organizations

The case study data reveal two major areas which have important implications for the management and design of voluntary organizations. One concern is that of management style and the other focuses on organizational design. It is not just the cases which prompt this analysis. The data from the wider sample also indicate that these are two of the most important factors for the management of voluntary organizations.

The clustering of the sample organizations into five strategic profiles largely rests on their orientation to strategy within their immediate domain (that of givers and receivers) rather than toward any wider or more macro context. Transformations in these organizations are largely achieved through the link between managerial decisions and the opportunities and constraints presented by the immediate organizational environment. More macro contextual factors, such as the position of the voluntary sector overall within the larger socio-political economy, seem to have little immediate impact upon managerial strategies. Our data examined a number of these factors (see Chapter 4) but none of them proved to be significant.

This is a finding worthy of some discussion. Wolfenden (1978) argued very strongly for the inherent flexibility of voluntary organizations which was not, in their view, being met at the time of the study. By flexibility, was meant the high levels of strategic discretion of the voluntary sector overall in relation to bodies such as the Government's Voluntary Services Unit, the independent intermediary bodies such as the National Council for Voluntary Organizations, and national and local government generally.

Whilst Wolfenden (1978) made reference to the management of voluntary organizations, they were only able to argue that it somehow had to get better (page 191) and progress from the 'aura of amateurishness' which characterizes it. The thrust of the Wolfenden analysis was at the systemic level of pluralism; the state in relation to the voluntary sector, the private sector in relation to the voluntary sector, and so on. Wolfenden spent little time in dealing with the practicalities of managing organizational strategies and change at the operational level.

This may, of course, reflect the historical context in which the Wolfenden Report was conducted. At the time, there were grave fears for the future of the voluntary sector as a whole. It was argued that the sector was facing a crisis of support and legitimacy and that, ultimately, survival meant successfully mediating between the public and private sectors.

A number of empirical and theoretical studies lent support to this view (see, for example, Leat *et al.* 1981), and the question of charitable status equally took centre stage as an example of government/voluntary sector inter-relationships (see Wilson 1984 and Gladstone 1982). At a more macro level of analysis we would argue that these issues are still of concern for the voluntary sector overall. We asked respondents about such issues in this study but their importance was rated as significantly less in relation to issues of the management process and the management of strategic change.

The reasons for this apparent shift of emphasis away from the macrosystemic to the actualities of operational management have come about not because the wider concerns are unimportant to managers of voluntary organizations (they are: see Wilson and Butler's 1985 study of the influence of central government agencies over decision making in the voluntary sector, for example), but because:

1. They are factors which lie largely outside the immediate control of individual managers irrespective of hierarchical seniority or organizational size. To change a socio-political system significantly it would need the concerted efforts of a great number of individual organizations acting together.
2. Since the mid 1980s, the voluntary sector overall has moved away from concerns of its own survival and legitimacy to the more individualistic concerns of efficient and effective management of specific organizations. Questions of competitive performance, strategic change, and professional management seem to be the keynote themes of the managers of individual organizations we talked to, rather than questions of state/voluntary sector relationships.

The data presented in this book indicate that the concerns of managers in the voluntary sector are probably for the first time very closely aligned with the concerns of their commercially based counterparts. Strategic survival and the continued regeneration of organization have become primary issues and, in order to achieve these, questions of organizational design and of management style have come to dominate the managerial agenda. The context in which these concerns have their focus is in the direct relationships with givers and receivers and not in the indirect relationships of systemic pluralism. Our data lend little support to the latter. Unless organizations fall into the reactor strategies (cluster 5), and this is only three charities from our sample, then the current strategic concerns of management seem to focus on the following key issues:

The management of interdepartmental interests and the disagreements which arise concerning what the organization should be doing, the services it offers and the relative application and apportionment of budgets.

The ability to sustain organizational flexibility with regard both to providers and receivers.

The design of integration mechanisms which facilitate effective communication throughout the organization and which can also serve as effective information systems.

The case studies, whilst of interest in their own right, are also designed to be mirrors which reflect the strategic issues and organizational concerns of the managers of the organizations in the wider sample.

Oxfam's concern with organizational image and its perception by external interests is shared by virtually all of the organizations in the extender cluster. Managers in British Red Cross, the Royal London Society for the Blind, and War on Want are all actively attending to issues of corporate image. These concerns are really reflecting a wider concern by these organizations to manage or 'enact' their operating environment (Weick 1969).

Although Christian Aid's case description is dominated by the management of structural change, its strategy of co-operation with other agencies is shared by all other organizations in its strategic cluster (competitive co-operators). Primary concerns of management here are focussed on maintaining co-operative links, but not at the expense of losing any competitive advantage to their sister charities. All organizations in this cluster are characterized by their competitive stance toward their environment. Competition is concentrated both at the level of securing inputs and providing services (outputs). These organizations might not be the leaders in their particular industry, but they are in a position to be influential in their sector of operations. Continued success for any of these organizations would most likely mean a shift into the extender cluster since competition would be overtly aimed at, and would operate on an even footing with the organizations in this cluster.

Royal National Institute for the Blind provides a case description of an organization which is trying to professionalize and to provide a more effective and efficient level of service. This is also characteristic of many of the other organizations in this cluster. Although the output co-operator cluster is the most diverse in terms of similarities between the organizations, one prevailing characteristic is that of stability. All the organizations already have or are developing stable relationships with receivers of services and other organizations.

It seems that demand for services is constant, so the key strategic issue for these organizations is providing outputs in a cost-effective way.

At the same time, none of these organizations is in a position to dominate any industry (as Oxfam does, for example), so cost effectiveness has to go hand in hand with achieving effective co-operation between other organizations in the field.

The four organizations in the acquisitor strategy cluster include RNLI, and each charity is characterized by a strategic orientation emphasizing the securing of funds in preference to other goals. The reasons for this strategy in RNLI have been discussed at length in this chapter, but Unicef, the Greater London Fund for the Blind, and British Wireless for the Blind equally display similar characteristics. They are all locked into long-standing and often formal relationships with funders, and the only real strategic choices which remain are those over inputs, since outputs are either predetermined or are not amenable to change without destroying the organization itself and starting again.

It is difficult to speak of the reactor cluster, exemplified by St Dunstan's, in the same manner as the other four clusters. Strategy here is of a different tenor and tone. It is notable largely by its absence and it is worth stating again that two of the three organizations in this cluster, St Dunstan's and the Scottish Institute for the War Blinded, seem unlikely to survive more than a few years.

Summary

It seems that the key issues facing charitable organizations today are those of effective and responsive management. More than ever before, concerns in the voluntary sector focus on the way in which the organization is managed. The inherent flexibility so often described as the hallmark of voluntary organizations now seems to be concentrated on the style and manner in which these organizations are managed. This involves both questions of internal management and of overall organizational design. It also concerns the strategic orientation of the organization and its ability or capacity to take on board the need to effect often quite radical changes in both strategic and operational elements.

The strengths of voluntary organizations can all too easily become pitfalls for the unwary. Since the moral overlays of altruism and voluntarism are so pervasive, the question of motivating staff largely becomes irrelevant. Many commercial organizations would be more than pleased to secure the level of commitment from employeees that is characteristic of the voluntary sector. However, there is a cultural problem which voluntarism brings with it. Employees expect a great deal of personal space, autonomy, and personal say in how the organization is run and over what should be its strategic goals. Currently, this is at odds with many of the management styles prevalent in voluntary organizations which are trying to develop and innovate their strategies.

Here, control and rationalization effected from the management perspective run counter to the rather individualistic culture of these organizations. The most 'natural' design of organization to accommodate both these concerns is the decentralized or the purely 'matrix' structure. Yet it is often overlooked that such structures have inbuilt in them tensions which demand precise and quite strictly controlled management and control systems. Thus, what initially seems natural can become a millstone which rather paradoxically mitigates against change and strategic development.

Voluntary organizations have come a long way since the relatively recent survey by Wolfenden in the late 1970s. The current research has indicated the major concerns of managers in the voluntary sector fall largely in the areas of professionalizing the management process and organizing the process of change without negating the strong cultural overlay of altruism and voluntarism. The management challenge that this scenario presents is immense, but it must be met if the voluntary sector is to flourish and regenerate in the changing context of the political economy of Britain into the 1990s.

Chapter eight

Strategy and structure: conclusions

If we were to identify one consistent theme throughout this book, it would be the sharply accelerating rate of change with which voluntary organizations must cope. Strategies and organizational structures must reflect the adaptive stance taken toward the environment in order to ensure survival and avert decline. The organizations in our sample have reflected manifestly different ways of adopting a strategic profile toward their immediate environment and we have identified empirically five clusters of strategy type. The case studies have reinforced this empirical distinction by isolating and identifying the detailed context in which strategies are formulated, changed, and reformulated in response to environmental demands.

The purpose of this chapter, however, is not merely to summarize what has preceded it. Rather, we shall develop some of the implications of our study for the management of voluntary organizations both now and in the future. Justification for this approach can be found in the data, of course. Organizations which adopt a strategy of doing nothing, or really defy any labelling of strategy *per se*, are approaching an era of decline from which they may never recover. St Dunstan's is an obvious example. Those organizations which will secure long-term survival are going to have to adopt a more proactive stance toward their environments even if this means that for the first time managers of charities recognize and act upon the wider political economy of which they are a part (Wilson 1989).

There are a number of key aspects which come out of the present study which will become pre-eminent issues for all charities if our sample is in any way representative. These may be summarized broadly under the following headings:

Managing organizational image
Managing the change process
Managing organizational culture and structure

Managing organizational image

Image is not a new concept for charities. They have always had to promote an image of some sort, although the emphasis with which image currently appears to be of concern has historically been concentrated rather more on convincing regulatory bodies that the aims of the organization were truly charitable (see Brooke 1984, Wilson 1984). The kind of image management which comes out of our data is largely unconcerned with charitable status but concentrates on managing the gift relationship. Inter-organizational dependencies have taken primacy and securing a set of givers (and convincing them why they should give) has become a key strategic issue for almost all active charities.

The implications of such a strategic shift effectively toward managing more actively the environment of givers are wide ranging and fundamental. There appear to be a number of trends discernible from this study in which the dual images of efficiency and administrative leanness surface as the key issues. Projecting an image of 'professional management' toward potential and existing givers has become almost ubiquitous from Oxfam to the Bible Lands Society. Many of the organizations in the sample had recently hired managers from outside the confines of the voluntary sector (for example, RNIB) with a view to translating assumed corporate management expertise into charity management.

Charities have always striven for an image of efficiency and part of this has been the projection of efficient and effective management, especially in the guise of administrative efficiency. Advertisements which emphasized the very small proportion of a donated pound which went into administrative overheads were testament to this (for example, Oxfam, War on Want, NSPCC). Thus a process of 'natural' professionalization has occurred over time and organizations have become much more efficient. Yet, the additional overlay of deliberately trying to import professional management skills and values is likely to have an impact on the wider context of charitable activity beyond that of increased efficiency. We outline these below. Such are their roots at the very basis of voluntary sector philosophy that such processes may well be irreversible.

First, the relationships between the state and charities will continue to take on a different perspective. Since the logical end point of professionalizing charity management is to increase their ability to stand alone as service providing organizations, the propensity of the state to offer complementary services will be reduced. 'Welfare pluralism' as proposed by Wolfenden (1978) and developed by Hatch and Mocroft (1983) is unlikely to persist in the domain of the political economy. As Gerard (1983: 146–8) notes, there are at least two reasons why this may be the case. The provision of welfare solely by the state, with any gaps filled by the voluntary sector, is untenable simply because of the complexity of modern society and the inability of state agencies to have the expertise or to provide the necessary coverage of service provision. Also, as voluntary organizations become visibly more professionally managed and visible, consumers will exercise their choice of 'exit' from the state provision of services (Hirschman 1970). They will view the voluntary sector as increasingly specialized but at the same time still expressive of values and beliefs not necessarily found in state agencies (Rothschild-Whitt 1979). Therefore, the tendency for voluntary organizations to be seen by the consumer as 'stand alone' providers of services will be increased and the reality of service provision solely by voluntary organizations will be secured in some areas.

Second, the context of the domain of voluntary activity will itself be subject to change. Each voluntary organization will be seeking to manage its domain in a way which secures distinctive competence in the services it provides. Along with professionalization will come a strategy of competition between voluntary organizations. We have already seen the seeds of this in the current book. In Third World aid and the visually handicapped sector, the level of competition between voluntary organizations is increasing. For the larger, established organizations this is probably not a bad thing. For the domain of voluntary activity overall, its benefits are less certain. Smaller charities are likely to be squeezed out as competition increases. The only tenable position of a smaller charity in this new strategic scenario is either to be a unique provider of services, or to be an adjunct to larger charities, such as the relationship between Road Runner and Oxfam described earlier in this book.

As Thompson (1967) and Miles (1980) argue, a domain characterized by competition between single organizational units is likely to result in a better and more efficient provision of some services, but it will seal the demise of others. Holes are likely to appear in the network of service provision as organizations seek out niches which are in demand, both from consumers and which are attractive to givers. Those niches which are less attractive and thus are not supported at a consistent level by givers will gradually cease to exist over time.

Macro-organizational theory would argue that this context favoured collaboration by some organizations. In other words, those organizations which were under threat from competition could secure a position of strategic advantage by teaming up with their peer charities which were in a similar position. Harrigan (1985) notes this process of joint venture or merger in the commercial sector under similar conditions. The problem in the British voluntary sector is that this seemimgly logical way forward is mitigated against by history and the way in which the charitable sector has grown as a separate legal entity. Charitable status, for example, has the unintended result of ensuring that organizations which are legally registered as charities remain separate entities. This is something rather peculiar to the British context. In the United States, the development of the notion of charities into non-profit organizations has lessened this organizational isolationism. As Heclo (1986) observes, whilst both Britain and the United States have been in the hands of governments which have favoured the reduction of state welfare provision, this has not hindered the development of non-profit organizations in the USA. Indeed, they have flourished both as gap fillers and as 'conglomerates' such as United Way which is also presenting something of a competitive threat to British charities in the aid sectors.

In Britain, the historical development of charities has not been distinguished by the same level of co-existence of state and voluntary activity. From the early part of this century, welfare provision became almost totally in the realm of state agencies (Rooff 1957). Voluntary organizations essentially set up in 'competition' with state agencies. Recent history has thus seen a cyclical see-saw of service provision either dominantly voluntary or mostly provided by the state. The effect of this has been to isolate individual voluntary organizations. Once they had established their niche, the tendency was to secure distinctive competence and not to engage in joint ventures or collaborate to any great extent with peer charities.

Today, this has resulted in many British charities, each of which is fiercely proud of its uniqueness. Current strategies toward handling the increasingly turbulent environment will exacerbate this isolationism as each organization tries to preserve its distinctive niche. The danger here lies not so much in voluntary organizations becoming more professional, but in their becoming increasingly inflexible so that when key contingencies change, their capacity to adapt quickly and effectively is severely reduced. Recent developments by some charities to try to secure an additional funding base from commercial organizations (or through partnership schemes with both local authorities and commercial organizations) also run the risk of inflexibility by increasing their strategic dependencies (Wilson 1989).

Managing the change process

Virtually all the organizations examined in this book are currently undergoing a period of change. It is also the most rapid and fundamental in their histories. As many authors have noted, the change process is often noted as long, difficult, and painful for participants. Pettigrew (1985) describes the tensions and protracted nature of securing change in Imperial Chemical Industries. De Man (1988) similarly details the agonies suffered by organizations in the Dutch context. There are countless other examples.

Seemingly, the key element of the change processes in the charities described in this book, especially those in Chapter 7, is that of reactivity. That is, the recognition of the need for change only seems to surface when the charity is in a state of near crisis or collapse. RNIB had been following a path of decline for some years until things began to get very serious for that organization and turnaround strategies were invoked. Christian Aid also had reached a point where something had to be done and the result was a massive change in organizational structure. With the possible exception of Oxfam, virtually all of the sample organizations show evidence of strategic inertia toward change, even many of those which are grouped in the extender cluster.

It is this inertia which is likely to place parameters on the often-argued flexibility of voluntary organizations (see Wolfenden 1978). Whilst the managers of voluntary organizations may be striving to increase efficiency and organization effectiveness, the relative neglect of managing the wider domain with its highly dynamic and interdependent nature will lead to restrictions on organizational autonomy and strategic stance (Thompson 1967).

This is not to say that achieving change in voluntary organizations will be facilitated solely by the recognition of their managers that it is necessary. Charities, like all other kinds of organization, are resistant to change. They are often conservative institutions with a heavy overlay of history and sometimes religious belief which together form a potent barrier to organizational change. As Robbins (1983: 283) says: 'In the battle between change and stability, bet on stability.'

Certainly, the theory of effective change in organizations espouses planned change. That is where forces for change (such as changes in funding bases, the entry of other organizations into the domain, or organizational performance loss and decline) are acted upon by a group of managers in the organization. In such a way, a proactive stance toward change is achieved. The danger in the sample organizations in this study appears to be the drive toward increasing specialization of service provision by each individual organization. If each charity becomes a totally unique provider of specialized services, then this too will create a large blockage to future change (Hage and Aiken 1970). The original flexibility inherent in a voluntary sector comprising loosely coupled organizations providing, for example, a general welfare service in child care of medical services will be lost as each organization strives for a distinctive role.

A further set of factors, which are particualarly applicable to organizations in the voluntary sector, will also have implications for the change process. In particular, the questions of organizational culture and structure will loom large as organizations adapt their strategies and orient themselves toward their domain. These are discussed in the next section.

Culture and structure in the voluntary sector

It was in Chapter 7 that the effects of culture and structure were discussed at length. In particular, we focused upon the need for voluntary organizations to professionalize and yet retain the values of altruism and motivate volunteering on the part of staff. In this final section, we shall develop some of the broader structural and cultural issues which seem to be of importance in the wider context of voluntary activity.

It seems that the massive changes in the role of the state, particularly since the Thatcher administration achieved power in 1979, have resulted in major changes for the voluntary sector. Over the last eight years, the state has been committed to a particular pattern in what Hirschman (1982) has termed the 'shifting involvements' of public, private, and voluntary activity. This pattern may be characterized by a major re-definition of the role of the state in welfare provision. The role of the voluntary sector is in the process of becoming more a stand-alone provider of services rather than as an adjunct to those provided by the state.

Whilst some commentators might see this kind of state policy as erosive, amounting to a certain kind of social Darwinism, it is not necessarily the case that public sector spending overall has been reduced. Rather the areas have been redefined largely away from welfare, education, and health to defence spending and the maintenance of law and order. Such shifts have also been true of the USA under the Reagan administration. The impact of these changes on the voluntary sector overall has been swift, fundamental, and possibly irreversible. The whole culture of voluntary activity is in the process of becoming re-defined and the task of charity managers is to meet this challenge without sacrificing the altruistic overlay of giving and volunteering.

The declining level of financial support from the state for voluntary organizations has averted some of the fears expressed by Leat *et al.* (1981) of the charities becoming mere extensions of state activity. But it has also brought with it the challenge of seeking new sources of funding and strategically positioning voluntary organizations to achieve a sustainable income. There have been some 'pots of gold' in the equation, notably in the form of securing monies from commercial organizations, but these have been beset with difficulties. As Wilson (1989) illustrates, only very few voluntary organizations stand to gain substantial and sustained income from commercial sources. Those charities in education, the arts and health are best placed, but others in Third World aid, visually handicapped, and general welfare are hardly supported at all.

Payroll deduction schemes, whereby individuals employed by commercial organizations can donate part of their salary to specified charities, have also yet to get off the ground as a major source of income for charities. Simlarly, partnerships between local authorities, commercial organizations, and the voluntary sector (especially in community-based projects such as housing and redevelopment) have yet to prove a significant funding base for charitable activity. Thus, increasingly managers of voluntary organizations are faced with creating, developing, and sustaining a funding base from the private individual, the voluntary donor of both time and money.

The changing dynamics of the culture and structure of the voluntary sector have sharpened the reality of managing the funding relationship for many organizations. For the first time, many voluntary organizations are beginning to examine the nature of the bequests, legacies, and gifts endowed to them in an attempt to systematize income data. For those organizations which can identify and sustain funding, the future looks promising. The opportunities to diversify services, to secure distinctive competence, and to compete in what has become the open market of charitable activity, have never been greater. For those organizations unable to fulfil these tasks, the future looks bleak.

The future

It is perhaps useful to examine our point of departure in this final section of the book. We began by noting that in theory charities had little justification for their existence. However, altruism and the strong human motive to donate gives the lie to purely rational theory. Charities do survive. Some grow and develop in quite a short time, by organizational reckoning, and household names like Oxfam and War on Want are the result. The future portrayed in this book is, however, quite different from that predicted by the last large-scale survey of the voluntary sector by the Wolfenden Committee (1978).

Wolfenden saw a voluntary sector co-existing with the state in a highly pluralistic manner, with a high degree of inter-organizational interplay between statutory and voluntary organizations. Ten years on, the interplay has been severely curtailed by the Conservativ   ent which was to come into power the year after the public   Now, the context is for voluntary organizations t a distinctive niche, and operate within it painted by Wolfenden was one in which i tions to overlap in service provision so th of choice available to the consumer' (Wolf have been curtailed as voluntary organi activities. Interestingly, Wolfenden pr income were such rationalization to occ Whether this is due to purely altruisti due to the sheer necessity of some v

172

to operate in the absence of any statutory provision of welfare is impossible to judge.

In one respect, the present study has borne out the recommendations by Wolfenden that voluntary organizations should engage in active 'self-appraisal' of their strategic activities and effectiveness generally (1978:191–2). Wolfenden's point stemmed from rather different assumptions than the last ten years have brought to pass, although the end results have been the same. In Wolfenden's pluralistic environment, greater organizational efficiency and effectiveness were means to an end. Greater levels of support could be gained, although there was an element of strategic choice in this, since those organizations which did nothing were assumed to survive. The current context portrays achieving efficiency and effectiveness as basic ends in themselves since without convincing potential givers of these aspects, organizational survival is at stake in the increasingly competitive charitable market.

A large part of this transition has been characterized by the desire of many voluntary organizations to recruit 'professional' managers into their ranks so that the competitive lessons learned in the commercial world can be translated into the charitable context. We have noted this process in a number of organizations. We have also noted how this seems to bring about an almost inevitable clash of values between voluntary staff, paid staff, and professional managers. At base level, this clash may result in a fundamental re-definition of the core values and ideology of the organization.

If this is to happen to any great extent over the next ten years, then the future of voluntary activity will change markedly. Citizens will find services provided only in those areas where organizations have been able to compete and survive. In other areas, it is likely that lacunae will occur in service provision and, for the first time since Beveridge, substantial gaps in welfare provision may be evident. We hope that the data examined in this book, although only a partial sample of the voluntary sector overall, give time for thought and reflection on the rapid changes which have already happened and will help preclude any further or future reduction in the range of services available through the voluntary sector.

Appendix to chapter three: a selection of some questions covered in the interview schedule

Operationalization of variables (*selected* to indicate areas covered)

1. Input strategy – towards givers

To what extent does each of the following describe strategies towards *securing inputs*?
Read through the statements first and rate each where:
1 = not at all, 2 = very little, 3 = somewhat, 4 = a lot, 5 = a very great deal.

1. Attempting to increase the efficacy of tested methods for securing inputs ⸻
2. Extending tested methods of gaining inputs to reach new givers ⸻
3. Developing new methods of securing inputs aimed at existing givers ⸻
4. Developing new methods of securing inputs to reach new givers ⸻
5. Enter into joint programmes of short/medium duration with other organizations in the same field ⸻
6. Enter into joint programmes of short/medium duration with givers ⸻
7. Have relatively stable relationships with other organizations in same field for securing inputs ⸻
8. Have relatively stable relationships with givers ⸻

2. Output strategy — towards receivers

To what extent does each of the following describe present strategy *towards clients/receivers*?
Read through the statements below and then rate each where:
1 = not at all, 2 = very little, 3 = somewhat, 4 = a lot, 5 = a very great deal.

1. Increasing efficiency in producing existing services   —
2. Extending delivery of existing tested services to reach new clients   —
3. Developing new services aimed at existing clients   —
4. Developing new services to reach new clients   —
5. Enter into joint programmes of short/medium duration with organizations in same field   —
6. Enter into joint programmes of short/medium duration with client groups   —
7. Have relatively stable and formalized relationships with other organizations in same field for service delivery   —
8. Have relatively stable and formalized relationships with client groups for service delivery   —

3. Lobbying

1. To what extent does organization lobby government(s) to create a more favourable environment? Circle as appropriate.
1 = not at all, 2 = occasionally for a specific purpose, 3 = frequently for many purposes, 4 = constantly.
2. Does any lobbying involve joining forces with other voluntary organizations? If so, which and for what?

4. Significant others in field

1. As regards this organization's inputs/outputs is it: (circle as appropriate)
   1 = virtually unique in its field?
   2 = nearly unique in a particular line of activity but there are some other organizations in a more general related field? — which organizations?
   3 = there are a small number of significant other organizations in the same field?
   4 = there are many organizations of significance in same field — give main ones.
2. What are the other significant organizations in the field?
3. How is field changing as regards entry/exit of other voluntary organizations?

5. Dependence

1. Consider the two largest single receiver groups who act independently of each other. Approximately what % of total spending goes to each?

Client 1 is .... spending .... %
Client 2 is .... spending .... %

2.   Consider the 2 largest single givers who act independently of each other. Approximately what % of total funds does each provide?

Client 1 is .... funding .... %
Client 2 is .... funding .... %

6. Operations

As regards actually *producing the outputs*, rank the following statements as to their accuracy in describing what happens. Where: 4 = most accurate, 1 = least accurate, 0 = inapplicable. Describe what actually happens under each. Different types can apply to different parts of the organization.

Routine: task presented *stable*, means of achieving it *well defined*.

Flexible/modular: task presented *variable*, means of achieving it *well defined*.

Craft: task presented *stable*, means of achieving it *unclear*.

Non-routine: task presented *variable*, means of achieving it *unclear*.

Norms

Rank the following statements as to their accuracy in describing the norms of the organization, i.e. rules and standards guiding behaviour, where: 4 = most accurate, 1 = least accurate, 0 = inapplicable. Try to explain in each case. If norms vary notably across different parts of organization note this.

Norms based upon commitment to an *ethical aim* or cause such as helping people with a problem. Rank   ——

Norms based upon development of *expertise* in a particular area combined with *service* to a client. Rank   ——

Norms based upon running a *well-organized, smooth-running* outfit with emphasis upon orderly procedures. Rank   ——

Norms based upon *efficient* use of resources in cost/benefit terms. Rank   ——

Structure

Specialization

A function is specialized when at least one person performs that function and no other function and when that person is not in the direct line command.

Appendix

Below is a list of functions defined in general terms that can be applied to any kind of organization. Work through the list giving each function a score of either 1 or 0, where 1 means that the organization has one or more specialists performing this task and 0 means that it does not.

Does this organization have one or more specialist employees to: Score

1. Obtain and control materials and equipment (buying, stock control) ___
2. Maintain and erect buildings and equipment ___
3. Record and control financial resources (accounts) ___
4. Carry outputs and resources/inputs from place to place (transport) ___
5. Control the quality of materials and equipment and outputs (inspection/monitoring) ___
6. Maintain human resources and promote their identification with the organization (welfare) ___
7. Control the workflow (production control) ___
8. Dispose of, distribute and service the output (sales and service) ___
9. Acquire inputs (e.g. fund raising) ___
10. Devise new ways of fund raising ___
11. Acquire and allocate human resources (employment) ___
12. Recruit/co-ordinate voluntary workers ___
13. Devise outputs, equipment, and processes (design and development) ___
14. Assess and devise ways of producing the output (methods) ___
15. Develop and operate administrative procedures (O & M) ___
16. Develop and transform human resources (training) ___
17. Develop, legitimize, and symbolize the organization's charter (public relations and advertising) ___
18. Deal with legal and insurance requirements (legal) ___
19. Acquire information on the operational field (market research) ___

Formalization

For each of the items, circle the number representing the appropriate score and enter this number against the item in the score column

Item   Score
1. Written contract of employment ___
2. Information booklets given to:
    none = 0, few employees = 1, many = 2, all = 3   ___

176

3. Number of information booklets:
   none = 0, one = 1, two = 2, three = 3, four or
   more = 4   ___
4. Organization chart given to:
   none = 0, Chief Executive only = 1, Chief
   Executive plus one other executive = 2, Chief
   Executive plus most/all department heads = 3   ___
5. Written operating instructions:
   not available to direct worker = 0, available to direct
   worker = 1   ___
6. Written terms of reference or job description for
   direct workers:
   not provided = 0, provided = 1   ___
7. For line (workflow) superordinates:
   not provided = 0, provided = 1   ___
8. For staff (other than line superordinates):
   not provided = 0, provided = 1   ___
9. For Chief Executive:
   not provided = 0, provided = 1   ___
10. Manual of procedures:
    none = 0, manual = 1   ___
11. Written policies:
    none = 0, written policies = 1   ___
12. Workflow (production) schedule or programme:
    none = 0, schedule = 1   ___
13. Written research programme or reports:
    none = 0, reports = 1   ___

Centralization

Score the following decisions with regard to the level at which they are
effectively authorized even if ratified at a higher level within the
organization.
Score on a scale of 0–6 where: 6 = above Chief Executive, 5 = Chief
Executive, 4 = Head of all workflow or in charge of one complete
output/fund or division, 3 = head of workflow sub-unit, 2 = supervisor,
e.g. field director, 1 = operator, e.g. field worker, 0 = collectively,
i.e. by all members of the organization.

Decisions   Score
                                                              0–6

1. Supervisory establishment   ___
2. Appointment of supervisory staff from outside the
   organization   ___

3. Promotion of supervisory staff   ——
4. Salaries of supervisory staff   ——
5. To spend unbudgeted or unallocated money on capital items   ——
6. To spend unbudgeted or unallocated money on revenue items   ——
7. What type or what brand new equipment is to be   ——
8. To determine a new product/service or programme (output) for client   ——
9. New method of fund raising   ——
10. To determine territories for aid/service   ——
11. To determine territories for fund raising   ——
12. The extent and type of clientele   ——
13. The extent and type of givers   ——
14. What shall be costed   ——
15. What activities should be monitored/inspected   ——
16. What operations shall be work studied   ——
17. Dismiss a supervisor   ——
18. Training methods to be used   ——
19. Buying procedures   ——
20. Which suppliers of materials are to be used   ——
21. What and how many welfare facilities are to be provided   ——
22. The price of an output   ——
23. The allocation of monies and other resources to programmes/projects   ——
24. Allocation of money to fund raising   ——
25. To alter responsibilities/areas of work of specialist departments   ——
26. To alter responsibilities/areas of work of operating departments   ——
27. To create a new department   ——
28. To create a new job   ——

Span of control

How many people report direct to the Chief Executive (or equivalent) whatever the status of the subordinate may be but excluding the Chief Executive's secretary?

Departmentalization

Of those reporting direct to the Chief Executive, give number whose *predominant job* is responsibility for tasks below. Number of people

given need not add to number in previous question because a person may
do more than one job.

(a) *Non-workflow staff*/advisory function (personnel,
     administration, advertising)   —

(b) *Workflow* but *NOT* a *complete product/service* (i.e.
     part of a wide operating process)
     titles: —

(c) *Workflow* and a *complete product/service* for
     delivering to clients (i.e. a product division)
     titles: —

(d) *Geographical area* (i.e. region of country or world)
     titles: —

(e) *Client sub-group* (i.e. a specified type of client as
     part of total clientele)
     titles: —

(f) *Project* of specific aim
     titles: —

Computation of departmentalization type

The raw departmentalization scores for each organization are: dl =
staff/advisory; d2 = process; d3 = product; d4 = area; d5 = client;
d6 = project

The adjusted departmentalization scores (D1, D2 – D6) are calculated
thus:

T (total score) = dl + d2 + d3 + d4 + d5 + d6

$$D1 = \frac{dl}{T}, \quad D2 = \frac{d2}{T} \quad\text{---}\quad D6 = \frac{d6}{T}$$

References

Aves, G.M. (1969) *The Voluntary Worker in the Social Services*, London: Allen & Unwin.

Blau, P.M. and Scott, W.R (1962) *Formal Organizations. A Comparative Approach*, London: Routledge & Kegan Paul.

Bradley K. and Gelb, A. (1982) 'The replication and sustainability of the mondragon experiment', *British Journal of Industrial Relations*, **10** (1), 20–23.

Brooke, M.Z. (1984) *Centralization and Autonomy: A Study in Organizational Behaviour*, London: Holt, Rinehart & Winston.

Burns, T. and Stalker, G.M. (1961) *The Management of Innovation*, London: Social Science Paperbacks.

Butler, R.J. (1983) 'Control through markets, hierarchies and communes: a transactional approach to organizational analysis', in A. Francis, J. Turk and P. Willman (eds) *Power, Efficiency and Institutions*, London: Heinemann.

Butler, R.J. and Carney, M.G. (1983) 'Managing markets: implications for the make or buy decision', *Journal of Management Studies* **20** (2), 213–33.

Chandler, A.D. (1963) *Strategy and Structure: Chapters in the History of the American Industrial Enterprise*, London: MIT Press.

Channon, D. (1973) *The Strategy and Structure of British Industry*, Cambridge, Mass.: Harvard University Press.

Chapin, F.S. and Tsouderos, J.E (1956) 'The formalization process in voluntary associations', *Social Forces*, **34**, 342–44.

Charity statistics (1985–6) 'Ninth Annual Edition' London: Charities Aid Foundation.

Chesterman, M. (1979) *Charities, Trusts and Social Welfare*, London: Weidenfeld & Nicolson.

Child, J. (1972) 'Organizational structure, environment and performance: the role of strategic choice', *Sociology*, **6** (1), 1–22.

Child, J. (1984) *Organization: A Guide to Problems and Practice*, London: Harper & Row.

Cyert, R.M. and March, J.G. (1963) *A Behavioral Theory of the Firm*, Englewood Cliffs, New Jersey: Prentice-Hall.

Deans, T. (1989) 'Organizing medical research: The role of charities and the state', in Alan Ware (ed.) *Charities and Government*, Manchester: Manchester University Press.

de Man, H. (1988) *Organizational Change in its Context*, Delft: Eburon.

Eccles, T. (1981) *Under New Management*, London: Pan Books.

Emerson, R.E. (1962) 'Power-dependence relations', *American Sociological Review*, **27**, 31–41.

Fitzgerald, M., Halmos, P., Muncie, J. and Zeldin, D. (1977) *Welfare in Action*, London: Routledge & Kegan Paul.

Galbraith, J. (1973) *Designing Complex Organizations*, Reading, Mass.: Addison-Wesley.

Gerard, D. (1983) *Charities in Britain: Conservatism or Change?* London: NCVO.

Gerlach, L.P. and Hine, L. (1970) *People, Power, Change: Movements of Social Transformation*, Indianapolis: Bobbs-Merrill.

Giddens, A. (1973) *The Class Structure of the Advanced Societies*, New York: Harper & Row.

Gladstone, F. (1982) *Charity Law and Social Justice*, London: Bedford Square Press.

✓ Hage, J. and Aiken, M. (1970) *Social Change in Complex Organizations*, New York: Random House.

Handy, C.B. (1976) *Understanding Organizations*, Harmondsworth: Penguin.

Hannan, M. and Freeman, M. (1977) 'The population ecology of organizations', *American Journal of Sociology*, **82**, 929–64.

Harrigan, K.R. (1985) *Strategies for Joint Ventures*, Lexington, Mass.: D.C. Heath, Lexington Books.

Harrigan, K.R. (1986) *Managing for Joint Venture Success*, Lexington, Mass.: D.C. Heath, Lexington Books.

Hatch, S. and Mocroft, I. (1983) *Components of Welfare*, London: Bedford Square Press.

Heclo, H. (1986) 'General welfare and two American political traditions', *Political Science Quarterly*, **101**.

Hickson, D.J., Butler, R.J., Cray, D., Mallory, G.R. and Wilson, D.C. (1986) *Top Decisions: Strategic Decision Making in Organizations*, San Francisco: Jossey-Bass and Oxford: Blackwell.

Hickson, D.J., Hinings, C.R., Lee, C.A., Schneck, R.E. and Pennings, J.M. (1971) 'A strategic contingencies theory of intraorganizational power', *Administrative Science Quarterly*, **16**, 216–29.

Hickson, D.J., Pugh D., and Pheysey, D.C. (1969) 'Operations technology and organizational structure: an empirical reappraisal'. *Administrative Science Quarterly*, **14**, 378–97.

Hirschman, A.O. (1970) *Exit, Voice and Loyalty*, Cambridge, Mass.: Harvard University Press.

Hirschman, A.O. (1982) *Shifting Involvements: Private Interest and Public Action*, Princeton, NJ: Princeton University Press.

✓ Johnson, N. (1981) *Voluntary Social Services*, Oxford: Basil Blackwell and Martin Robertson.

Kanter, R.M. (1972) *Commitment and Community: Communes and Utopias in Sociological Perspective*, Cambridge, Mass.: Harvard University Press.

References

Kanter, R.M. (1979) 'The measurement of organizational effectiveness, productivity, performance and success: issues and dilemmas in service and non-profit organizations', *Program on Non-profit Organizations*, working paper, no. 8: Yale University.

Kanter, R.M. (1983) *The Change Masters: Corporate Entrepreneurs at Work*, London: Allen & Unwin.

Katz, D. and Kahn, R.L. (1966) *The Social Psychology of Organizations*, New York: Wiley.

Kimberly, J.R., Miles, R.H. and Associates (1980) *The Organizational Life Cycle*, San Francisco: Jossey-Bass.

Knight, K. (1974) 'Matrix organizations: a review', *Journal of Management Studies*,13 (2), 11–30.

Lawrence, P.R. and Lorsch, J.W. (1969) *Organization and Environment*, Illinois: Irwin.

Leat, D., Smolka, G., and Unell, J. (1981) *Voluntary and Statutory Collaboration: Rhetoric or Reality?* London: Bedford Square Press.

Lehmbruch, G. (1977) 'Liberal corporatism and party government', *Comparative Political Studies*, **10**, 91–126.

Lehmbruch, G. (1982) 'Neo-corporatism in comparative perspective', in G. Lehmbruch and P.C. Schmitter (eds) *Patterns of Corporatist Policy Making*, London: Sage.

Leontiades, M. (1980) *Strategies for Diversification and Change*, Boston: Little Brown.

Leviathan, V. (1984) 'The kibbutz as a situation for cross-cultural research', *Organization Studies* **5** (1), 67–75.

Lindblom, C.E. (1959) 'The science of muddling through', *Public Administration Review*, **19**, 79–88.

Masson, G. (1986) 'Public perceptions of Oxfam', *MBA Dissertation*: University of Warwick.

Mauss, M. (1954) *The Gift*, New York: Norton.

Merton, R.K. (1957) *Social Theory and Social Structure*, Glencoe, Ill.: Free Press.

Meyer, J.M. and Rowan, B. (1977) 'Institutionalized organizations: formal structures as myth and ceremony', *American Journal of Sociology*, **83** (2), 340–63.

Miles, R.H. (1980) *Macro-organizational Behaviour*, Santa Monica, Ca.: Goodyear.

Miles, R.E. and Snow, C.C. (1978) *Organizational Strategy, Structure and Process*, New York: McGraw-Hill.

Mintzberg, H., Raisinghani, D., and Theoret, A. (1976) 'The structure of "Unstructured" Decision Processes', *Administrative Science Quarterly*, **21**, 246–75.

Moyer, M. (ed.) (1983) *Managing Voluntary Organizations: Proceedings of a Conference Held at York University, Toronto*, Toronto: Faculty of Administrative Studies.

National Council for Voluntary Organizations (1983) 'Government influence on voluntary organizations', *Working Paper*, London: Bedford Square Press.

National Council for Voluntary Organizations (1984) 'Relations between the

Voluntary Sector and Government: a code for voluntary organizations', *Working Paper*, London: Bedford Square Press.

Nightingale, B. (1973) *Charities*, London: Allen Lane.

Ouchi, W.G. (1980) 'Markets, bureaucracies and clans', *Administrative Science Quarterly*, **25** (1), 129–141.

Parton, N. (1981) 'Child abuse, social anxiety and welfare', *British Journal of Social Work*, **2**, 391–414.

Perrow, C. (1970) *Organizational Analysis: A Sociological View*, Belmont, California: Wadsworth.

Peters, T. and Austin, N. (1985) *A Passion for Excellence: The Leadership Difference*, London: Guild.

Peters, T. and Waterman, R. (1982) *In Search of Excellence: Lessons from America's Best Run Companies*, New York: Harper & Row.

Pettigrew, A.M. (1979) 'On studying organizational cultures', *Administrative Science Quarterly*, **24** (4), 570–81.

Pettigrew, A.M. (1985) *The Awakening Giant: Continuity and Change in Imperial Chemical Industries*, Oxford: Blackwell.

Pettigrew, A.M. (ed) (1987) *The Management of Strategic Change*, Oxford: Blackwell.

Pfeffer, J. and Salancik, G.R. (1978) *The External Control of Organizations: a Resource Dependence Perspective*, New York: Harper & Row.

Pfeffer, J. and Nowak, P. (1976) 'Joint ventures and interorganizational interdependence' *Administrative Science Quarterly*, **21** (3), 315–39.

Porter, M.E. (1980) *Competitive Strategy: Techniques for Analyzing Industries and Competitors*, New York: Free Press.

Porter, M. (1985) *Competitive Advantage: Creating and Sustaining Superior Performance*, New York: Free Press.

Pugh, D.S., Hickson, D.J., Hinings, C.R., and Turner, C. (1969) 'The context of organizational structure', *Administrative Science Quarterly*, **14**, 91–114.

Quinn, J.B. (1980) *Strategies for Change: Logical Incrementalism*, Homewood, Ill.: Irwin.

Robbins, S.P. (1983) *Organization Theory: The Structure and Design of Organizations*, Englewood Cliffs, N.J.: Prentice-Hall.

Rojek, C. and Wilson, D.C. (1987) 'Workers' self-management in the world system: the Yugoslav case', *Organization Studies*, **8** (4), 297–308.

Rokeach, M. (1968) *Beliefs, Attitudes and Values: a Theory of Organization and Change*, San Francisco: Jossey-Bass.

Rooff, M. (1957) *Voluntary Societies and Social Policy*, London: Routledge & Kegan Paul.

Rothschild-Whitt, J. (1979) 'The collectivist organization: an alternative to rational bureaucratic models', *American Sociological Review*, **44**, 509–27.

Saxon-Harrold, S.K.E. (1986) *Strategy in Voluntary Organizations*, Unpublished Ph.D. thesis: University of Bradford.

Saxon-Harrold, S.K.E., Carter, J., and Humble, S. (1987) 'The charitable behaviour of British people: a national survey of patterns and attitudes to charitable giving', Charities Aid Foundation, London.

✓ Scott, D. (1982) *Don't Mourn For Me - Organise: The Social and Political Uses of Voluntary Organizations*, London: Allen & Unwin.

Shanklin, W.L. and Ryans, J.K. Jr. (1981) 'Is the international cash cow really a prize heifer?', *Business Horizon*, **24**, 10–16.

Simon, H.A. (1956) *Administrative Behaviour*, New York: Macmillan.

Smiles, S. (1898) *Self Help*, New York: A.L. Burt.

Snow, C.C. and Hambrick, D.C. (1980) 'Measuring organizational strategies: some theoretical and methodological problems', *Academy of Management Review*, October, 46–58.

Streeck, W. and Schmitter, P.C. (eds) (1984) *Private Interest Government: Beyond Market and State*, London: Sage.

Swords, M. (1987) 'Which way now? a study of Oxfam, its supporters and its future strategy', *MBA dissertation*: University of Warwick.

Thompson, J.D. (1967) *Organizations in Action*, New York: McGraw-Hill.

Tillotson, K. (1954) *Novels of the Eighteen Forties*, London: Routledge & Kegan Paul.

Titmuss, R. (1970) *The Gift Relationship: From Human Blood to Social Policy*, Harmondsworth: Penguin.

Tonnies, F. (1955) *Community and Association*, London: Routledge & Kegan Paul.

Tsouderos, J.E. (1955) 'Organizational change in terms of a series of selected variables', *American Journal of Sociology*, **20**, 206–10.

Udy, S.H. (1965) 'Comparative analysis of organizations', in J.G. March (ed.) *The Handbook of Organizations*, Chicago: Rand-McNally.

Weber, M. (1947) *The Theory of Economic and Social Organization* (Trans. and Ed. A.M. Henderson and T. Parsons), Glencoe, Ill.: Free Press.

Weick, K. (1969) *The Social Psychology of Organization*, Reading, Mass.: Addison-Wesley.

Whipp, R., Rosenfeld, R., and Pettigrew, A.M. (1987) 'Understanding strategic change processes: some preliminary British findings', in A.M. Pettigrew (ed.) *The Management of Strategic Change*, Blackwell: Oxford.

Williamson, O.E. (1976) *Markets, Hierarchies: Analysis and Antitrust Implications*, New York: Free Press.

Williamson, O.E. and Ouchi, W.G. (1981) 'The markets and hierarchies and visible hand perspectives', in A.H. Van de Ven and W.F. Joyce (eds) *Perspectives on Organization Design and Behaviour*, New York: Wiley.

✓ Wilson, D.C. (1984) 'Charity law and the politics of regulation in the voluntary sector', *King's Counsel*, **34**, 36–42.

Wilson, D.C. (1989) 'New trends in the funding of charities: the tripartite system of funding', in A. Ware (ed.) *Charities and Government*, Manchester: Manchester University Press.

Wilson, D.C. and Butler, R.J. (1985) 'Corporatism in the British voluntary sector', in W. Streeck and P.C. Schmitter (eds) *Private Governments as*

Agents of Public Policy, London: Sage.

Wilson, D.C. and Butler, R.J. (1986) 'Voluntary organizations in action: strategy in the voluntary sector', *Journal of Management Studies*, **23** (5), 519–42.

Wilson, D.C. and Rosenfeld, R.H. (1989) 'Cultures and co-operatives', in P. Khandwalla (ed.) *Organizational and Behavioural Perspectives for Social Development*, Calcutta, India: Sage.

Wolfenden (1978) *The Future of Voluntary Organisations: Report of the Wolfenden Committee*, London: Croom Helm.

Author Index

Subject Index

Action Aid 89, 91; public
  perception of 152
altruism 2, 52
Armitage, Dr Thomas Rhodes 116

Band Aid 21
Beeching, James 131
Bible Lands Society 89, 95, 96, 97
Booth, William 13
British Council of Churches 108
British Leprosy Relief Association
  84, 85
British Red Cross 23, 77, 80, 81;
  public perceptions of 152
British Wireless for the Blind 98,
  99, 100, 102
Bruce, Ian 121, 152

Catholic Agency for Overseas
  Development 89, 93
change: active and passive
  responses to 148–9, 169; and
  organizational identity 162; and
  organizational life cycles 150;
  and the trend to de-centralize
  150–3; and values 153–5, 157;
  conflicts between individual and
  organizational attitudes; in
  organizational culture 122, 153,
  154, 163, 164, 170; in strategy
  115, 149, 160, 161, 165–72; in
  structure 108–13, 149, 158–60;
  pressures for change 126, 148,
  149; the motivation of
  individuals 163–4; the role of

crisis 152, 168, 169; the role of
  leaders as orchestrators 113,
  114, 121, 141, 142, 152, 155
Charitable Trusts Act (1853) 7
Charitable Uses Act (1601) 7
charities: and context 51, 52, 167,
  168; history and development
  11–13, in the mixed economy
  10–11; legal definition 6–9
Charities Act (1960) 7
Charities Aid Foundation 4
Charity Commission, the role of 6,
  8, 9, 19, 29
Charity Information Bureaux 9
Child Poverty Action Group 8
Christian Aid 27, 84, 86, 87, 121;
  case description 108–16; changes
  in organizational structure,
  background 108–13; major
  sources of income 110;
  organizational structure 28;
  public perception of 152;
  strategy 112, 114, 115
Comic Relief 21
Council for Voluntary Services 16
Council for Voluntary Youth
  Services 8

Elliot, Charles 108
Environment of the organization:
  co-opting 53; coalescing 53;
  contracting 52; givers and
  receivers 58; institutional environment 49, 50; lobbying activity
  74, 75; significant others 54

188